The 'Modern Writers' Series

Other titles in this new series of short guides to contemporary international writers:

Already published

SYLVIA PLATH	**Eileen Aird**
V. S. NAIPAUL	**William Walsh**
SOLZHENITSYN	**Christopher Moody**
PHILIP LARKIN	**David Timms**
HAROLD PINTER	**William Baker and Stephen E. Tabachnick**

In Preparation

ROBERT LOWELL	**J. F. Crick**
GÜNTER GRASS	**Irène Leonard**

J. M. Cohen

Jorge Luis Borges

BOOKS
10 East 53d St., New York 10022
(a division of Harper & Row Publishers, Inc.)

Oliver & Boyd

Croythorn House
23 Ravelston Terrace
Edinburgh EH4 3TJ
A Division of Longman Group Limited

ISBN 06-491252-3

Printed in Great Britain by
Cox & Wyman Limited,
London, Fakenham and Reading

To
J. L. and Elizabeth Gili

In memory of pleasant conversations in the days of Hitler's war, in which I first heard the name of Jorge Luis Borges.

Publisher's Note

Except where otherwise stated the author has himself translated the excerpts of Borges' work appearing in this book—quotations from poems being taken from first versions.

Contents

Introduction   1

1   Buenos Aires, Geneva, Madrid, and again Buenos Aires   5

2   The Streets of the Capital   14

3   The Argentinian Scene   23

4   Towards a Crisis   36

5   *Ficciones*   50

6   More *Ficciones*   64

7   The 'Mystical' Experience   78

8   Shrouded Mirrors   86

9   Survival of a Poet   99

10   Borges in his World   104

Bibliography   113

Introduction

Jorge Luis Borges is one of the few contemporary writers universally known. Paperback editions of his *Ficciones* and *El Aleph*, the
two volumes of stories on which his fame rests, can be bought in
half a dozen translations throughout the Western world, though
the communist world ignores him, disliking his values. For this
seemingly mild and scholarly writer is a controversial figure and
largely, as will be seen, it was he who started the controversies. A
writer so widely read has in the past generally had a wide range
of work to his credit. But Borges' reputation rests on these two
books alone. The rest of his work—poetry, essays, prose sketches,
a biographical sketch and various works written in collaboration
with others—remain almost unknown and untranslated. Recently a bilingual selection of his poems has appeared in London
and New York; and some of these will no doubt help to broaden
the base of his reputation. But on the whole, it is fair to say that
the poems lead up to and away from the two famous volumes. By
the light of his early poetry we see the growth of those ideas which
give the stories their profound originality; and in the later poetry
we see a man growing reconciled to the uncertainties that he
did not succeed in resolving in his crisis years, an aging poet,
almost blind when he is suddenly overwhelmed by worldwide
acclaim.

The stories were written in the Forties and the acclaim came
in the Sixties. A large proportion of his readers, indeed, were
unborn when the stories were written. Prophetically he understood the situation of a generation then unthought of, which has
come to doubt the metaphysical assumptions of its fathers and
grandfathers.

Borges is a man who doubts all men's certainties, even his own,
a man who clings to his unbelief in the belief that only in unbelief
can certainty be found. The paradox is deliberately Borgesian.

The stories are parables of possible belief either in the meaning-fulness or the random unreason of the world. They are fantasies, built from an ironical rag-bag of curious reading, convoluted speculation, and the deductive techniques of the detective novel. They are original, though Borges himself claims as ancestors Poe and de Quincey, Chesterton, R. L. Stevenson and H. G. Wells. These stories are inimitable, though Borges considers that younger men have plagiarised him. As will be shown, he has set an example to many younger writers in Spanish America, but all have pursued their own courses. He has been for them an influential point of departure.

Borges is an important writer not for his breadth, but for the depth and individuality of his thought, the immense accomplishment of his Argentinian language, and the magnificent economy and construction of his stories. His writing is Argentinian, not only in his obviously un-Castilian sentences and turns of phrase, but in its dependence on a broader cultural heritage than that of Madrid. He has a wide acquaintance with literature, English, German, French, Latin, Greek and old Scandinavian. He seldom mentions Spanish authors, only Cervantes and the bitter seventeenth-century poet Quevedo who, like him, saw the foundations of his world sinking.

Borges is a pessimistic ironist, but at the same time an Argentinian patriot. 'These fragments I have shored against my ruins', he seems to say of his stories, and the ruins are exactly located in the huge, characterless city of Buenos Aires, which has now largely replaced the characterful colonial city of his childhood. Never was a writer of international fame more locally rooted in a place far distant from the centres of civilisation, yet open, by way of its few fine writers, to all the currents of thought and influence of the northern hemisphere. If Argentina hardly existed in the world's eyes before Borges wrote of her, she is now recognisable as a country with a familiar past, and this she owes to the work of Borges.

This book would not claim for him the greatness of Tolstoy or Dostoevsky, who familiarised the world with their country. Length is not everything, but the narrowness of Borges' interests and sympathies—the corollary of their intensity—ranges him in the ranks of the lesser masters, beside Poe, Fitzgerald, de Quincey and Kipling. Even today, when we are not liberally blessed with greatness, his Chilean neighbour Pablo Neruda dwarfs him by the breadth and range of his poetry, by his humanity, his humour and even by his faults of vulgarity. Neruda is to Borges like Victor Hugo to Théophile Gautier, like a volcano to a chiselled pyramid. But in Borges' pyramid too there smoulders a fire, deliberately damped by the ironic springs of his uncertainty.

Though Spanish America has greater poets than Borges, and latterly some story-tellers of far greater scope, his achievement gains by its purposeful narrowness an intensity that we rarely find in contemporary writers. He himself might think of Kafka, whose short stories he has translated, as a peer. But the contrast between the Czech and the Argentinian master of ironic doubt is very great. Kafka's anxiety is personal, a haunted apprehension of guilt and estrangement embodied in a fictional world of nightmare simplicity. Borges' existential anxiety is metaphysical, and projects itself in fables that embody philosophical hypotheses. Borges has the lightness of an intellectual who can conjure away his fears by sheer play of thought and association. His stories are perhaps a kind of spell; they preserve his doubts but stifle his anxieties by a game of elaboration. If there is no sure reality, he seems to say, then there can be no unreality either. If life is a dream, who is dreaming that dream, and who is dreaming the dreamer? If there is a God, who created that God, and who created the creator? Borges delights in those religious heresies that plant such questions. Invariably he prefers a heresy to a faith, and an intellectual game of suppositions to any statement of fact, Borges makes a game of time and space, of eternity and nothingness, constructing his own rules by reference to the philosophers, to Plato and Spinoza, Berkeley and Hume, Schopenhauer and Nietzsche. But philosophical speculation is in his eyes a game also, and a philosophical theory is an artistic construction of the same seriousness or frivolity as a story or a poem.

Borges' stories therefore are games of invention, modelled on those of the gods, existent or not, when they created the existent or non-existent worlds. This Borges allows, in those interviews that he gives so freely and in which he gives so little away, but he has also said many times that every one of them is founded on his own experience. To relate the stories and Borges' other work to

3

his experience, to reconcile the public and private figures of Borges, symbolised by him as 'Borges' and 'I' is perhaps the prime aim of this book. To achieve it, I shall guide the reader through the little known work of the poet's early years—he was thirty-eight when he began to write the *Ficciones*. Many of these poems are, I believe, remarkable for their own sake, and not merely as premature statements of themes developed in the stories. The first two chapters are a necessary introduction to the mature Borges. He himself, though compulsive in his frequent renunciations of his own past, has lately begun to restore to favour poems that he had once decided never to reprint.

In his habit of disowning his own past achievements, Borges may remind one of our own Robert Graves. There are other resemblances. Both poets are essentially myth-makers; both have searched the byways of legend and speculation for tales that suit their preconceptions of the world. Both are fascinated by the writings of the Sufis, and by the underground religious tradition that they claim to represent. Perhaps some unhappy graduate searching for a subject for his thesis may one day decide on a joint study of Graves and Borges as 'two Sufi poets'. This thesis would be no more extravagant than some that have appeared recently in the United States, where Borges studies have now become an industry. Indeed, in our own university of Cambridge, Borges was asked to comment on an examination question on the subject of his own work. With his habitual interviewee's coolness, he neatly turned the examination question on its head. To be the subject of scholarship cannot but amuse a writer who has made such play with scholarship. A catalogue of Borges' literary allusions in his stories and essays would include a fair number of fakes and a number of others used out of context. For his assumption of scholarship is another of his games. Actually he has read only what has pleased him for wholly Borgesian reasons, and plucked picturesque passages from books that he would never have had the patience to read, even had his eyesight allowed.

Now let us turn to Borges' life and writings, in an endeavour to discover the rules of his highly original game.

1 Buenos Aires, Geneva, Madrid and again Buenos Aires

In the year 1914, shortly before the outbreak of the First World War, an Argentinian lawyer, Jorge Borges Haslam, brought his family to Europe for their education and for the cheaper living to be enjoyed there. The family consisted of his wife Leonor Acevedo, their elder child Jorge Luis, a delicate and short-sighted boy of fourteen, his sister Norah, and their grandmother, born Frances Haslam, who had come out from Burslem and married an Argentinian officer, soon to be killed in the Civil War against the dictator Rosas. After a stay in Paris and a tour of Northern Italy, the Borges family settled in Geneva, where they remained throughout the war.

The Borges family were 'oligarchs', the sons and grandsons of landowning gentlemen who had served as officers in the War of Independence against Spain, in the frontier campaigns against the Indians, in nineteenth-century wars against Argentina's neighbours and on the Conservative side against Rosas. Their more distant ancestry was probably Portuguese, perhaps partly Jewish, but ancestral memories did not stretch back beyond the War of Independence. The fourteen-year-old Jorge Luis' ancestors and his grandmother's Northumbrian forebears played a great part in the formation of his mind. He spoke and read English, and at the age of nine had made a translation of Oscar Wilde's 'Happy Prince' which had been printed in a Buenos Aires newspaper. Already the boy's ambitions were to be a writer. His father, whose legal practice had never occupied much of his time, also had literary ambitions. He brought with him to Europe an unfinished novel, printed subsequently at his own expense.

The Borges family were cultivated South Americans, of a kind frequently to be met in Europe before 1914. They differed from many, however, in the strength of their ties with their homeland. Jorge Luis had been born in the city of Buenos Aires, but the family had moved two years later to a large house in the suburb of Palermo, the smallest details of which remained printed on the future poet's imagination. Palermo was then a suburb of strong contrasts. There were new houses with large gardens like that of the Borges, and there were shacks inhabited by picturesque ruffians, a criminal fringe of toughs and strong-arm men, the bodyguards of local politicians, and the heroes of legendary knife-duels among themselves. From the shacks, the boy could hear the plucking of the guitar and the ballad accompaniment of the 'payador', singing improvised verses on local events in an unde-clamatory Argentinian Spanish. The boy's parents forbade him to visit the shacks, or to wander beyond them into the Pampa, the great limitless plain that begins at the edge of Buenos Aires and extends almost unbroken to the Andes and to Patagonia. From the windows of the Borges mansion, the young Jorge would watch the vast red sunsets over the Pampa, which gave him a strange intimation of infinity. The family house, the shacks and their inhabitants, and the vast sunsets of the plain possessed the boy's imagination throughout his years in Europe, and recurred in his poetry and stories throughout his productive years.

Geneva, the ceaseless Rhône and the Lake along whose banks he walked to school, meant less to the poet and recur but seldom in his poems. But the education that he received and the friends he made there affected him greatly. The teaching was, of course, in French, a language which the boy hardly knew. Indeed he had the greatest difficulty in keeping up with the lessons at the excellent college where he took his *Baccalauréat*. Jorge Luis' enthusiasm was for English, in which he was already very well read. In his father's library he found de Quincey, R. L. Stevenson, Wilde, Chesterton and a good deal of history and philosophy. French authors attracted him less and though he wrote his first poems, now lost, in that language, he has always been a great enemy of the conventional Parisian orientation of Argentinian culture. At school he was so well grounded in Latin and Greek that the *Odyssey* and the *Aeneid* became familiar books to him.

Books and intellectual discussion were Jorge Luis' principal, almost his exclusive, interests. At school in Buenos Aires, he had been bullied by his tough and unintellectual comrades. In Geneva he was happier. A Jewish classmate, Maurice Abramovitz, introduced him to Rimbaud's poetry, and he himself decided to learn German, attracted by Schopenhauer and by the Expressionist poetry which had originated in pre-war Germany and which, as the war went on, was taking an increasingly pacifist and revolutionary tone. The young Borges read the fragmentary and explosive poems of August Stramm, Wilhelm Klemm and the rest, which he was later to translate and to imitate in Spanish. In German too he met Whitman for the first time, in an expressionist translation. He also read a German best-seller of that period, Gustave Meyrinck's *Das Golem*, the retelling of the seventeenth-century legend about a rabbi in Prague who made a mechanical man. The mature Borges wrote one of his finest poems on this subject, which is closely akin to that of his own *Ficciones*.

Jorge Luis' leanings towards Expressionism were natural to the time and place. In wartime Switzerland Dada was born, James Joyce was writing, and some of the Expressionists themselves had taken refuge. At a café table in Zurich, Lenin is said to have played chess with Tristan Tzara, two revolutionaries in their different spheres, political and poetic, who would have had no language in common. That even Jorge Luis, the well brought-up son of a very close Argentinian family, should have been infected with the new ideas current in 1917 and '18 is not surprising, though the mature Borges always tried to minimise, even to deny them. In neutral Switzerland, as in the rest of Europe, the Russian revolution, the defeat and collapse of Germany, the influenza epidemics and food shortages engendered an apocalyptic excitement, especially among intellectuals. In Jorge Luis' case, however, there was from the start a strong counter-influence, that of his Argentinian family tradition and of a greater preoccupation with the past than with the future or even with the present. At the end of the war, he was reading the gaucho poets of the nineteenth century, Argentina's sole original writers, who were to remain of prime interest to him throughout his life. These poets of the towns had written outstanding narrative poems about the gauchos of the plains, cattle men and at times rustlers, of mixed Spanish and Indian descent, who represented for Borges, together with the strong-arm men of Palermo, the real Argentina. He saw these poems as his country's epics, its minor *Iliad* and *Odyssey*, and the language in which they were written seemed to him in those days the true Argentinian Spanish.

An Argentinian traditionalist, a timid young man with much reading and poor eyesight, Jorge Luis Borges had from the outset a preoccupation with violence and violent men. The gaucho poems, the legendary knife-duels of Palermo, and the stuttering machine gun fire imitated in the syncopated cacophonies of the Expressionists, all fed this turbulent side of his imagination.

In 1918 the Borges family moved to Lugano, and next year to Spain. In Spain, they settled first at Barcelona, then at Palma de Mallorca, where Jorge Borges Haslam had his novel printed in a form much elaborated by his expressionist son, whose linguistic extravagance he both admired and regretted. Towards the end of his life he is said to have wanted to print the novel afresh in its original form. It was not a book of great value, nor was Jorge Luis' first book of poems, written at this time in praise of the Russian revolution and entitled either *Ritmos rojos* or *Salmos rojos* ('Red verses' or 'Red psalms') which was not published and has long ago been destroyed by its author. Some stories of this period, written in imitation of Pio Baroja, have also disappeared; the only one submitted to a periodical was rejected. Towards the end of 1919, the family moved to Seville, where Jorge Luis met various *avant-garde* poets, and contributed to a number of short lived magazines. His first published poem 'Al mar' ('To the Sea') is a Whitmanesque dithyramb.

From Seville, the Borges family moved to Madrid, where Jorge Luis, now twenty, met most of the leading writers, took part in the customary all night *tertulias* (evening parties for intellectual conversation) at the leading literary cafés and acquired a considerable reputation as a propagandist for and translator of the Expressionists.

By the year 1921, the revival of letters which had begun in Spain in the last years of the nineteenth century was running into decline. Beginning with the defeat by the United States in 1898, it had now reached a second moment of national disaster, the catastrophes in Morocco. The first generation of 'Modernists' had drawn their poetic inspiration from France, their philosophical ideas from Germany. But nothing specifically Spanish had emerged except a constant preoccupation with 'the Spanish Question', with the reasons for the country's decline and with the possible remedies, nationalist, Marxist, internationalist that were open to it. The principal achievements of the first twenty-five years of intellectual recovery lay in the field of liberal and secular education. Spain had now a new generation of intellectuals, and the Madrid café life that Jorge Luis entered in 1921 was lively, though still provincial.

The first generation of modernist poets had revived Spanish literature by recourse to French models. *Modernismo*, in Spain and Spanish America, followed the line of French symbolism and parnassianism. The syntax, the long rhetorical *vers-libre*, the expanded Latinate vocabulary were French; they echoed Verlaine and his lesser followers, however, learning little from the concentration of the greater French poets, Baudelaire, Mallarmé, Rimbaud. Of the leading Spanish writers, Unamuno stood apart, a traditionalist more deeply indebted to the English nineteenth century than to the French; and Antonio Machado pursued a lonelier, more provincial course, uninfluenced by Madrid fashions and himself influencing no one.

The impresario of the new poets whom Jorge Luis met, first in Seville and then in Madrid, was an eccentric talker and framer of manifestoes, also a minor poet, Rafael Cansinos Asséns. It was he who devised the title *Ultra*, first for a soon defunct magazine published in Oviedo, then for the rather more long-lived Madrid periodical which gave its name to the whole poetic movement of reaction from modernism. For Ultraism was not a poetic movement but a reaction from French styles, and those most closely identified with it, like Cansinos Asséns, were minor writers or, like Borges, men who soon drifted out of Ultraism's orbit. The young men of 1921 had read Rimbaud and the new French poets of the war years, Guillaume Apollinaire, Max Jacob, Pierre Reverdy and Georges Ribemont-Dessaignes; they had a distant interest in Dada and in the Italian Futurism of Marinetti, and they admired the eccentric Ramón Gómez de la Soma, a writer of witty and trivial prose sketches and a figure of café life as compelling in his monologues as Cansinos Asséns. Borges was attracted to Cansinos Asséns, but after a long sitting at Ramón Gómez's table, decided that he was a bore, and did not return.

The young Borges' contribution to the Ultraists' conversations was an enthusiasm for the Expressionists and a knowledge of philosophy. He was already fascinated with the problems of reality and illusion and could quote relevantly from Berkeley, Hume, Spinoza and Schopenhauer, and from stranger writers, such as Swedenborg and the Kabbalists. His enthusiasm for the Russian revolution had evaporated. Now he was more concerned with revolutions in the arts. But already he appears more sober and intellectual, more reflective and better read than the rest of the Ultraists. He retained his preference for English above French, and fostered his Argentinianism. However much at home in Madrid or Barcelona, a Spanish American never identifies himself with Spain. He is conscious of belonging to a wider world, more open to London, New York and Paris itself. He feels the Pyrenees to be claustrophobically high. But for the moment, Borges was immersed in the literary world of Madrid.

Ultraism was a reaction and a literary ferment, and it is hard to derive any consistent programme from its frequent manifestoes. It is, however, quite simple to discover what Ultraism meant to the young Argentinian by reference to an article and anthology which he contributed in 1921 to the Argentinian journal *Nosotros*. He sums it up under four heads:

1. Reduction of the lyric to its primal element, the metaphor.
2. Removal of bridge passages, connectional and useless adjectives.
3. Abolition of ornamental flourishes, self-relevation, circumstantial detail, sermonising and contrived nebulousness.
4. Synthesis of two or more images in one, thus increasing their power of suggestion.

Poetry is thus reduced to a succession of powerful but disconnected metaphors. The metaphor is for Borges the core of the poem, and it was for their metaphors that he anatomised his fellow poets in the reviews which he published in *Ultra* and other organs of the sect. Jorge Luis Borges himself signed a handful of poems, of which he reprinted one or two in his first published collection, *Fervor de Buenos Aires*, only to remove them in later editions. Two can be quoted as representative. The first 'La trinchera' ('The Trench') is in the expressionist manner and could be mistaken for a translation from the German.

> Anguish.
> High above a mountain is moving forward.
> Earth-coloured men sink like wrecked ships into the
>   deepest fissures.
> Fatalism yokes the souls of those
> who bathed their hope in the fonts of night.
> Bayonets dream of nuptial thrusts. The world is lost,
>   and the eyes of the dead are seeking it.
> Silence is howling on the sunken horizons.

By Borges' own standards the metaphors are not remarkable. The poem is literary, lacking the stuttering immediacy of a battle piece by Stramm, its probable model. Bathing their hopes in the font of night produces a telescoped image of night's coolness, the pause in the battle and the holy water in the font suggests the illusions of religious faith. But the most original line in the poem is the Argentinian 'entreveros nupciales', a foretaste of the full Argentinian vocabulary of Borges' style of the mid-Twenties.

The next poem, 'Singladura' ('Day's run of a ship') conforms better with the ultraist postulate of the condensed metaphor.

> I have plucked the violin of a horizon well-lip of the
>   world where the sun lies in soak
> The wind sculpts a succession of waves
> The mist blurs sunsets
> The night spins round like a wounded bird
> In my hands
>   The sea
>   comes to die
> The cathedral-like sea
> welded of spires and stained glass
> The half-moon has coiled itself around a mast.

Here the metaphors are chiefly visual and not well related to one another. The poem is an intellectual conceit so compressed as to be puzzling rather than illuminating. The condensation is excessive and, at the poem's opening, the comparison of the horizon to a violin string, the transition from tactile to visual imagery is rather too abrupt. The young Borges had certainly not succeeded in adapting the expressionistic metaphor to his descriptive purpose. In fact the adaptation of these forms of European modernism to Spanish poetry was successfully undertaken by another South American poet who frequented the Madrid cafés at the same time as Borges. This was the Chilean Vicente Huidobro, whose *concionisme* was closely related to Ultraism. But Huidobro was a poet of far greater scope than Borges, and far more closely related to his French contemporaries. Indeed he wrote some of his poetry in French. Huidobro's long poem 'Altazor' can be thought of as the culmination of Ultraism. It circulated in manuscript during Borges' stay in Madrid. But in his discussion of Ultraism, he does not refer to it.

In conversation with his Madrid friends, Jorge Luis dismissed his years in Switzerland as tiresome, constricting and leading nowhere. Switzerland was a country of drizzle. In the same way, on falling under the influence of the Spanish Ultraists, he renounced his enthusiasm for Whitman. For if poetry was by definition lyrical and brief, and a poem was no more than an assemblage of new and striking metaphors, the vast, untidy incantations of *Leaves of Grass* failed to fulfil the denfinition. The German Expressionists got by, since they were at least brief and immediate. But already Borges' critical sense had matured. His definition of Ultraism just quoted contrasts demonstrably with others attempted in the various Ultraist magazines, and even more strongly with the confusion of the editor of one of them who, asked in a café for a definition of Ultraism, turned to Cansinos-Asséns, who was fortunately present, and said 'You tell him!' Many of the Ultraists were ignorant and ill-read. Borges, though he easily renounced his Swiss education, was capable of profound aesthetic speculations which went far beyond the facile improvisations of his Madrid friends. Already, in an essay published in *Ultra* of May 1921, he saw beyond Ultraism: metaphor, that verbal arc, almost always traces the shortest line between two spiritual points.

The poet's aim is clearly expressed. But despite his explicit rejection of metaphysics, the attempt to convey the *sensation in itself* is a metaphysical one. It recalls Keats' remark in a letter of 1817: 'O for a life of sensations rather than thoughts.' Re-reading the poem 'La singladura', already examined for its striking but ill-coordinated metaphors, we cannot accept it as an account of sensations immediately conveyed and stripped of emotional overtones. The plucking of a violin-string, and the wounded bird, are melancholy, as is the falling rhythm of the poem itself. Only the wind sculpting the procession of waves suggests an immediate impression unqualified by poetic mood. The poem in fact is impressionistic and sad, but broken up by some very contrived metaphors. The basic model is the impressionistic poet, Juan Ramón Jiménez, whose melancholy seascapes, composed half-a-dozen years earlier, were influential with many poets Spanish and American. Despite his very different poetic practice, Juan Ramón had declared himself an advocate of a complete poetic change and the Ultraists accepted him as a precursor, even as a sympathiser with their programme.

Other poems contributed by Borges to *Ultra* come even closer to the impressionistic model of Juan Ramón Jiménez. But this master's influence could not cure him of his schematism. The poems are too theoretical. While they are more carefully reasoned than those of his fellow Ultraists, they utterly fail to convey the immediacy that was his aim.

Nevertheless, when he left Spain to return home in 1921, he left a reputation that lasted until his brief return a year or so later. To his Spanish friends, he appeared to have gone only to spread the gospel of Ultraism in the republics of South America. And indeed he went a convinced Ultraist with the intention of founding Ultraist groups and magazines in his native Buenos Aires.

2   The Streets of the Capital

Jorge Luis Borges and his family returned to the capital of their country, from which they had been absent for seven years. To the young poet it was a return not to the real Buenos Aires, an imitation Paris of straight intersecting streets, fine shops and Edwardian baroque buildings that lies between the Plaza de Mayo and the Plaza San Martín, a city which had prospered by its trade with the Allies, capital of a country that seemed to be emerging from an era of semi-colonialism to become a counterpart of the United States in the southern hemisphere. The Buenos Aires to which the poet returned was the city of a dream fostered during his European exile. His affection was for suburban streets remembered from childhood, for the shacks inhabited by roughs and prostitutes on the edge of Palermo, for the lurid night-town around the Paseo de Julio, and for the colonial buildings, the old cemeteries and the painted façades at the street corners, pink, blue or green, which were a feature of those shabby suburbs.

> The streets of Buenos Aires
> are the inner being of my soul.
> Not the energetic streets
> wracked with bustle and exhaustion
> but the gentle street of the suburb.

These opening lines of Borges' first book of poems, *Fervor de Buenos Aires* of 1923, set the scene. The general mood of this poem is between nostalgic and celebratory, the language impressionistic, though broken up by Ultraistic metaphors and unusual words. The version of 'Las calles' printed in present editions has been purged of its Ultraisms, as have other poems in the collection. 'Enérgicas', 'prisas' and 'arrabal' have disappeared, as has the ugly redundancy 'de mi alma'. The poem reads more smoothly, the substituted words and phrases are more colloquial, but the flavour of a young man's poem has vanished.

Borges' affection for the streets of Buenos Aires has been life long. When I first met him in 1953, I asked him which were the streets that he wrote of in his poems. We started on a long walk, the reason for which I supposed to be his fear of arrest by Perón's police, who were in those weeks rounding up the intellectuals. I learned afterwards that it was his custom to take his acquaintances on long walks, during which he pointed out a church with a tiled dome—reminiscent of Valencia or of Puebla in Mexico—an arcade or row of painted shops, a grilled gate through which a Spanish-type patio could be glimpsed, with a fountain and pots of herbs and scarlet geraniums or begonias—the courtyard of the poem 'Un patio', another of Borges' pieces which he now prints in changed and abbreviated form. I quote the middle section.

> Courtyard, canalised sky.
> The courtyard is the window
> through which God looks on souls.
> The courtyard is the slope
> down which the sky pours into the house.

In the revised version the second of these conceits disappears. The other two remain unchanged. In this poem can be seen the beginnings of Borges' mythologising of his native city. It is significant that the reference to human souls is the one to disappear from the poem. Borges is more concerned in *Fervor de Buenos Aires* with streets than with their inhabitants. Indeed, at the end of 'Calle desconscida' ('Unknown street') he has to remind himself

> Secret and tender
> was the miracle of the bright street,
>   and only later
> did I realise that the place was strange,
> that every house was a candelabra
> on which lives burn each with a separate flame,
> that every unpremeditated step we take
> treads in other men's Golgothas.

translation by W. S. Merwin

15

This poem too has been re-written but this final statement remains almost unchanged. But the removal of *ajenos* ('other men's') from the last line weakens it, for the effect of that adjective is of compassion, and it humanises the moral of the poem.

The mystery of other men's lives, of the unknown Golgothas upon which any chance step may ignorantly tread, is most strongly suggested in this book by a poem on the dictator Rosas, the enemy of Borges' aristocratic ancestors, whom they overthrew in battle and who ended his life in exile. The poet hears the tyrant's name pronounced in the quiet sitting-room of his parents in an age that lacks the 'adventures and alarms' of Rosas' day and reflects on the obliterating hand of time, which reduces historical figures to the ordinariness of 'you and me'.

> Perhaps Rosas
> was just a greedy dagger, as my grandparents said.
> But I believe he was like you and me,
> a chance card slipped into the sequence of events,
> that he lived in daily anxiety
> and disturbed the uncertain lives of the rest,
> bringing them either joys or griefs.

Borges was already moving, during his early years in Buenos Aires, away from impressionistic landscape and Ultraist conceit towards those philosophical themes that were to be the prime subject of his maturity. Already in 'La Recoleta', his first poem on the subject of the cemetery which contained his ancestral tombs and would in the end contain his own, he reflected on time and mortality and personal survival.

> Kindly shadow of the trees,
> wind with birds that billows over the branches,
> a soul dispersing among other souls,
> it would be a miracle if at some time they should
>   cease to be
> an incomprehensible miracle,
> although the idea of their repetition
> may soil our days with horror.
> These things I thought in La Recoleta, the place of my
>   ashes.

Here we have the first statement of Borges' permanent dilemma. He would wish the soul of the dead to disperse among other souls, but he is haunted by the fear, by the intuition that there is in fact another life on earth, a reincarnation or a return to re-live the life that has ended. The idea of re-birth terrifies him, that of oblivion and dispersal is a comfort. In later poems and in many of the stories of *Ficciones* and *El Aleph*, this basic dilemma is faced afresh with varying degrees of horror. Borges believes despite himself in the repetition of lives. His constant prayer to the God who, he hopes, does not exist, is: 'Alas, I believe. Strengthen my unbelief.' Already in *Fervor de Buenos Aires* we meet the fervent agnostic who cannot obliterate his intuitional faith.

In the two years between Borges' return and the publication of this first book of poems, he devoted himself to the propagation of Ultraism in Argentina, promulgating the four points quoted in the last chapter and gathering a few young people who, unable to raise sufficient funds to found a magazine, printed their poems on placards, which they stuck up at night on the capital's walls and billboards. The sheets were generally torn down next morning. But they gained the young Ultraists an invitation to contribute to existing magazines and after a year they were able to found their own, which they entitled *Proa* (*The Prow*).

Borges found Buenos Aires extremely provincial. As Madrid was to Paris, so was Buenos Aires to Madrid. A small reading public rapidly accepted and forgot the latest European styles much as rich Argentinian ladies bought and discarded the latest Parisian fashions displayed in the stores on Florida. But nothing specifically Argentinian was evolved, and the poetic scene was dominated by the country's great bad poet Leopoldo Lugones, a Victor Hugo of *modernismo*, who himself adopted and discarded a variety of styles and subjects, and a variety of opinions ranging from art-for-art's-sake to an admiration for dictators. Lugones had the gift of exuberant language, the power of adopting other men's styles and turning them to grand effect. In *Lunario sentimental* (*Sentimental Moon-Book*) of 1909 he laced the thin but individual wine of Jules Laforgue with crude *caña*—the cane brandy of Argentinian bars. In 1910 he hymned the centenary of independence with Whitmanesque optimism, and later exploited gaucho themes in ballads that were at least less vulgar than his modernist borrowings. Lugones bestrode the poetic world. He was the 'verbal gymnast' of the age and his dominion was not openly challenged. In fact Borges never came openly out against him. In apologising for his rather thin study of a minor poet, *Evaristo Carriego* (1930) he remarks that he would have done better to write of someone more important, Lugones for instance. But in the first chapter of his eventual study of Lugones (1955) he quotes so many bad lines and phrases as to sink the poet under the weight of his ridicule. Yet Borges has never been willing to condemn Lugones outright, seeing him if not as a major poet at least as a great national force. As a patriot Borges accepted the 'verbal gymnast', since with him Argentina acquired a great figure indeed one who claimed to have been a co-founder of *modernismo*.

'In contrast to the barbarous United States', Borges wrote in an introduction to an anthology of Argentinian poetry of which he was co-editor (1941) 'this country (this continent) has not produced a writer with world influence—an Emerson, a Whitman, a Poe—or even a great esoteric writer—a Henry James or a Melville. But we certainly have a few poets not inferior to those of any other Spanish-speaking nation. It is sufficient to mention the names of Lugones, of Martinez Estrada, of Banchs!'

The last two are minor poets conservative in form and restricted in theme, certainly unfit to be compared with the poets whom Borges had known and read in Spain—Unamuno, Antonio Machado and Juan Ramón Jiménez. Patriotism distorted the young poet's vision, and even to the last in 1960, in the introductory note to his miscellany *El hacedor* (*The Maker*) he drew an imaginary picture of himself presenting a copy of his book to the grateful Lugones, who had been dead for more than twenty years. In fact the two men never liked one another. Lugones did not welcome new talents, and Borges disliked exuberance of language and claims. Nevertheless he continued to respect Lugones as a national phenomenon, and excused his barbarism.

Soon after his arrival in Buenos Aires, Borges met an almost unknown writer, who came to influence him and whom he influenced. Macedonio Fernandez (1874–1952), a counterpart to Rafael Cansinos-Asséns, was a bohemian of the cafés who wrote poems and short prose pieces of great aesthetic sensibility, few of which were published. Indeed in his perpetual migrations from boarding house to boarding house most of them were deliberately left behind. Macedonio did not value his writings, which were, however, carefully gathered by Borges and his friends and subsequently published. He would not count as a man of letters, were it not for his position as leader of the *avant-garde*, who saw in his pronouncements an anticipation of Ultraism. An extreme idealist, he learnt philosophy from Borges, welcomed his news of the avant-garde movements in Europe, and in return fostered the young man's *criollismo*—his enthusiasm for things Argentinian— and encouraged him in the creation of his myth of Buenos Aires. Macedonio was the opposite of Lugones, a man of no achievement, but of great intellectual fervour, of great sensitivity and honesty and of devotion to his friends. When Borges met Macedonio, he commented many years later, he was 'credulous', accepting all that he read. Macedonio taught him to be critical and sceptical. Macedonio was a prime influence with the young Ultraists, and when they founded *Proa*, though not strictly of their number, he was appointed co-editor.

For the young Borges this grey-haired spell-binder was not a philosopher, but the incarnation of philosophy. He was a *Zaddik*, that is not one who comments on the Jewish law but the Law in person. So he wrote thirty years later on the occasion of Macedonio's death after several spells in mental hospitals. Macedonio was unaffectedly Argentinian, an admirer of the gaucho poets, and a natural metaphysician. His most brilliant and drollest judgements arose spontaneously at the café table and were, as Borges remembers, probably somewhat spoiled in the writing down. He was passionate yet free from self-dramatisation, and refuted the ultimate reality even of the self. 'I suspected', adds Borges, 'that he denied the self in order to protect it from death, since if it did not exist death could not touch it.'

In retrospect, in this memorial article for Macedonio, Borges speaks of the 'dry and greedy poems that he (Borges) wrote during the week in the mistaken manner of the Ultraist sect, and the justification of that week in the café conversation of each Saturday night.' In fact the poems of *Fervor de Buenos Aires* were far from dry, and in what way they were greedy it is hard to say. Perhaps he meant that they were greedy for fame. Macedonio's greed was, in

contrast, so small that he wrote very little and generally abandoned his manuscripts.

A second important influence on the young Borges was the
poet and scholar Alfonso Reyes (1889–1959), at that time Mexican
ambassador in Buenos Aires. Reyes, like Borges, came of military
stock and was culturally a traditionalist. He entertained Borges
to lunch every Sunday and their discussions covered a wide range
of mutual interests. In the immense body of Reyes' critical essays,
Borges' name occurs frequently, and Reyes quotes seriously his
rather brash views—expressed in the early essays—on Góngora,
whose Latinised mythologising he rejected. Reyes and he indulged
in discussion and correspondence on the subject of Argentinian
phrases, the detective novel and various philosophical problems,
all greatly to the advantage of the young poet, who must have
contrasted Reyes' sobriety and his deep and accurate reading with
the eccentric genius of Macedonio Fernandez, whom Reyes regarded as one of the last in the line of Hispanic eccentrics, a man
without a following but with a certain influence. We do not find in
Reyes' work any reference to Borges' early poetry.

His first volume, *Fervor de Buenos Aires*, was printed in an edition
of 300 copies at his own expense, the usual practice of South
American poets, and distributed not by the bookshops but by the
poet himself who, having given copies to his friends, devised an
original plan for achieving a wider circulation. He persuaded
the editor of an established literary periodical to have copies put
into the overcoat pockets of all his visitors, as they hung in the
lobby outside his office. Thus Borges gained the attention of a
number of his fellow writers and secured some notices in other
periodicals. In retrospect, Borges views with pleasure those days
when 'nobody thought about literature in a commercial way and
nobody expected to be paid' (Interview with Alex Zisman,
Cambridge Review vol. 93 No. 2207, May 1972). The implication is
that in the days when the poet wrote with no hope of a larger
audience than that of a few friends, he 'wrote for his own satis-
faction'; now he is concerned with making a literary success and
tempers his work to the market.

Fervor de Buenos Aires would have been the same book under any
publishing conditions. It is uneven, a young man's book, in
which not all the experiments succeed and in which the influence

of the Spanish Ultraists is not entirely absorbed into a personal style. Its best poems are metaphysical arguments, the weaker are impressions of the city. The latter are informed by a vague melancholy, by the longing for a conventional life of the last century, and for a bride waiting for him in a quiet room leading from one of the patios into which the poet gazed in his perambulations of the city. Some of these poems have disappeared from recent editions. Such metaphysical pieces however as 'Amanecer' ('Daybreak'), a speculation on the Berkeleyan theme of reality owing its existence only to the presence of spectators, survive, though with a certain paring of adjectives and ultraist conceits.

'Amanecer' in its original form has a power of metaphysical reflection that proves the young Borges to have been much more than an elaborator of dry confections 'in the manner of the sect'.

> If things are devoid of substance
> and if the populous city of Buenos Aires
> like an army in its complexity,
> is no more than a dream,
> produced by many souls in common alchemy,
> there is a moment
> when its existence is in particular danger
> and this is the tremulous moment of dawn
> when sleep breaks down the activities of thought
> and only a few night-strollers preserve
> the ashen and vaguely outlined
> vision of the streets
> that they will afterwards redefine with all the rest.
> Hour in which the persistent dream of life
> is in danger of breaking,
> reduced with inevitable anguish
> to the narrow channel of a few souls still thinking,
> hour in which it would be easy for God
> entirely to destroy existence, which is now half-dead!

A philosophical disquisition, but at the same time an early statement of Borges' fear of non-being, of annihilation, that came nearest to him in insomnia, in sickness and in his habitual night wandering through the suburbs of Buenos Aires. The poem has been twice revised, and each time has become a little flatter, the more unusual adjectives being deleted or replaced with epithets less arresting. Like Borges' other poems in this volume they benefit rather than lose by their Ultraist surprises.

In returning to his native city Borges renounced his years in Europe just as in coming to Madrid he had renounced his education in Switzerland.

> This city which I believed was my past
> is my future, my present;
> the years that I lived in Europe are an illusion,
> I have always been (and shall be) in Buenos Aires.

Thus he ends the poem 'Arrabel' ('Suburb'). Europe was to be forgotten, as indeed for many years it was. Nevertheless, after barely two years at home Borges made a second journey there, revisiting Spain, touring particularly in Andalusia, and stopping in Paris and London, where he had few friends. Paris he found particularly alien to him. London he loved for its associations with his favourite English authors, with Keats at Hampstead, with de Quincey wandering at night through the Soho streets, with Chesterton, who at the time could still have been found in his favourite Fleet Street pubs, with James in Chelsea and Sherlock Holmes in Baker Street. But Borges was not to see London again for forty years.

3 The Argentinian Scene

On returning from his European trip Borges refounded the magazine *Proa*, which for a time prospered, even acting as a publishing house for the books of young poets. But his primary task on arriving back in the New World was to define his own attitude to the Argentine tradition, indeed to define the Argentine tradition and its language.

In *Fervor de Buenos Aires*, he had been content to transplant the Ultraism of Madrid, and to use his native city as a backcloth to the drama of childhood remembered and of the alienated poet wandering familiar and haunted streets. But now arose the question of national identity. He had been content to use Argentinian phrases and the features of the capital decoratively. He had always loved the gaucho narratives of the nineteenth century. But for the rest Argentina had no native writers except the abundant Lugones. The gaucho poems used local turns of phrase, even local orthography. But they were a sport, half a dozen poems written by townsmen on the subject of the ranchers and their quirkish resistance to the domination of townsfolk and central government. *Martín Fierro* was a great poem. But it established no tradition. If Borges was at first tempted to characterise its author as the Argentinian Homer, he soon moderated his views.

What is Argentina? Poets in the United States were asking similar questions in the same decade. The poems of Edgar Arlington Robinson and Robert Frost were dramatic lyrics and monologues in the Victorian tradition. Only the local colour was American. Carl Sandburg, on the other hand, used the rhythms of American speech, aiming to continue from the point reached by Walt Whitman, the only great poet his 'barbarous' country had produced.

The rhythm of *Fervor de Buenos Aires* was *vers-libre*, somewhat stricter than that of France and similar to that of other poets writing in Spanish, in the various countries of America. The Spanish poetic revival of the Twenties and Thirties was more traditional. Coinciding with the rediscovery of Luis de Góngora at his tercentenary in 1927, it had its roots far more deeply planted in the seventeenth century than was possible for an Argentinian. Borges admired the black sonnets of Quevedo. But Quevedo was no closer to him than were Shakespeare or Donne.

The magazine *Martín Fierro*, founded in Borges' absence, had come out with a flaming manifesto in favour of Argentinianism. The organ of Ultraists, Futurists, and others who believed that 'everything is new under the sun', it called for 'a great slash of the scissors at all umbilical cords.' It proclaimed its belief in all that was Argentinian; language, customs, viewpoint, and the capacity to absorb and assimilate all influences from abroad. But what precisely was the Argentinian language? That it differed from the Spanish of Madrid and Seville was obvious. The basic intonation was different. It differed too from the Spanish of the other American republics. But hitherto literary Argentinian had had little character of its own. Extremists among the *Martín Fierro* group proclaimed that the true Argentinian was *lunfardo*, the thieves' jargon of the slums. Others looked to the gaucho poets or to the gauchos themselves and their songs to the guitar for examples of the country's true idiom. Borges was carried some way on this nationalistic current, and in his second book of poems, *Luna de enfrente* (*Moon across the Way*, 1925) made use of many conscious Argentinianisms which he afterwards claimed to have found in a dictionary. He also modified the spelling of many words to conform to the spoken inflexion. In this he went no further than Juan Ramón Jiménez in Spain, who adopted a spelling to suggest the Andalusian sound. But in later printings of *Luna de enfrente*, Borges reverted to normal spelling and replaced his Argentinian words with more conventional Spanish.

In a recent introduction to a reissue of the book, for which he evinces a considerable distaste, he contrasts its more public and 'ostentatious' character with the more intimate quality of *Fervor*. In fact, most of its poems follow the general tenor of those in his earlier book, dwelling more insistently perhaps on the haunting and obscurely menacing character of its suburban streets under the moon. One meets for the first time in 'Calle con almacen rosada' ('Street with a pink shop') that particular corner, encountered on a chance walk, which he later used for the setting of his tale of knifings and lechery 'Hombre de la esquina rosada' ('The Man at the Pink Corner'). The place though seen for the first time had a ghostly familiarity:

> Here once more is the certainty of the pampa
> on the vague horizon
> and the waste lot vanishing into weeds and wire
> and the shop as bright
> as last evening's full moon.
> The street corner is as familiar as a memory
> with those long kerbs and the promise of a courtyard.
> How pleasant to bear witness to you, eternal street,
>   while my days have still looked upon so little!

The poem is impressionistic. The hint of *déjà vu* is hardly pressed home, and the reflection in the last line quoted is somewhat flat. What the poet appears to be saying is that he is glad to have received the impression of this street corner on the edge of the city at a time when his mind has not yet been flooded with experiences. The poem seeks to capture the memory of a significant moment, of a hint of eternity in the midst of time, which is a constant theme of Borges' poetry and of his subsequent stories and metaphysical speculations.

As for the 'public and ostentatious' aspects of *Luna de enfrente*, these are combined in a historical ballad 'El general Quiroga va en coche al muere' ('General Quiroga rides to his death in a carriage'), a poem which Borges chides for its Argentinianisms ('al muere' for 'a la muerte') and accuses of having 'the showy beauty of an oleograph'. With this epithet, he could equally demolish the whole *Romance gitano* of García Lorca.

The poem uses the metre of the traditional Spanish *romance* to tell the story of a general in a nineteenth-century civil war, carried to his execution in a coach over the desolate pampa. The language is rich and self-conscious, almost self-mocking, as if the poet found this tale of a historic killing faintly ridiculous. For he over-whelms it with contrived Argentinian phrases used rather as the Spanish poets of the seventeenth century, Quevedo in particular, encrusted their *romances* with *germanía*, the thieves' jargon of their century.

> Alongside the postillions a black man was galloping.
> To ride to your death in a carriage—what a splendid
>   thing to do!
> General Quiroga had in mind to approach the haunts
>   of death
> Taking six or seven companions with slit throats as
>   escort.
>
> That gang from Cordoba, trouble-makers, loud-
>   mouthed, shifty,
> (Quiroga was pondering) now what can they possibly
>   do to me?
> Here I am strong, secure, well set up in life
> like the stake for tethering beasts to, driven deep in the
>   pampa.
>
> *translation by* Alastair Reid

The poem is a baroque achievement. But Borges had no baroque ambitions. Indeed he wrote only one other poem in this manner, the decorative myth of the foundation of Buenos Aires ('Fundición mítica de Buenos Aires') which is equally successful in the neo-seventeenth-century manner.

In the first years of his permanent return to Buenos Aires, Borges wrote a number of essays, contributed to various periodicals and subsequently collected in three volumes: *Inquisiciones* (*Investigations* 1925), *El tamaño de mi esperanza* (*The Extent of My Hope* 1926), and *El idioma de los argentinos* (*The Argentine Language* 1929). These three books, published in small editions, have never been reprinted. Borges has indeed waged a ceaseless war against them, buying up any copies that have reached the second-hand book-stalls of Buenos Aires and even on occasion asking his friends' permission to destroy copies that he found on their shelves. When in the mid-Fifties he agreed to the publication of his 'complete works' his chief reason was, he tells us, in order to decide once and for all what was to be excluded. They contain views from which Borges now strongly dissents. There is even an attack on Whitman, a poet whom Borges has greatly admired since the Twenties, but who was no doubt unacceptable by Ultraist standards since metaphor played an unimportant part in his verse. Borges also engaged in literary polemics, especially in *El idioma de los argentinos*, in which he considered various contemporary Argentinian writers, on whom he was most severe. Long afterwards in 1953, when I asked him what contemporary Argentinian writers I should read, he recommended only Martínez Estrada's poetry. The same question ten years later produced the answer 'None'.

The three books of essays show Borges establishing his position in relation to three main topics. Many of them, he tells us, owe their origin to conversations with Macedonio Fernandez. In the first place, we see his advance from Ultraism—the elaboration of single images, which confined a poem to lyrical length—to the consideration of metaphor as the total myth of a poem, a viewpoint or analogy by which the poet expressed his whole conception of the world. For metaphysically the world can only be expressed in terms of the imagination. This was the second of Borges' subjects of inquiry in the three suppressed volumes. Adopting the Berkeleyan standpoint, already attractive to him in Madrid, he denied the reality of being. Nothing existed, according to this argument, apart from the percipient. The percipient, for Borges, was the artist. The social or psychological personality was unimportant. On the creative being alone nature depended for its existence. The theme is expressed poetically in the poem 'Amanecer' quoted in the last chapter. For at dawn, when there are few percipients in the streets, the whole city is in danger of disappearing. But Borges carries his nihilistic speculation still further and rejects the notion of time, even of eternity, as an expression of duration. History is for him an eternal repetition of the same events, which recur almost without variation. This idea must be considered later in reference to the essay on 'cirular time'.

The consequences of these speculations (for Borges' writing) were very great. Firstly, if there is no time and no being apart from the percipient, the moment of vision—described in the poem as a kind of *déjà vu*— is all important. Appearances are a kind of

27

multiple mirror reflection. But, at a given moment, many images flow together; a street or a house are seen in depth, not in time but in recurrence, in their repeated existences. Therefore the poem must be brief, or must expand from a single brief vision, which would itself be a metaphor for reality. But a metaphor could not be a mere elaborate fancy. It must conform to the poet's perception, his belief. Thus, discussing Shakespeare's sonnet *CVII* in *El idioma de los argentinos*, Borges writes,

> Shakespeare begins a sonnet thus: *Not mine own fears, nor the prophetic soul of the wide world dreaming on things to come. . . .* The experience here is crucial. If the phrase *prophetic soul of the wide world* is a metaphor, it is only a verbal flourish or merely a personal generalisation; if it is not a metaphor, if the poet really believed in the existence of a common, universal soul of this world, then the phrase is truly poetic.

Later Borges modified this argument and, with Coleridge, postulated not the poet's belief in this entity, but a mere suspension of disbelief during the process of creation.

The third subject of the three early books, the nature of Argentinianism and of the Argentinian language, served chiefly to divorce the poet from Europe. Ultimately, he decided that to write self-consciously as an Argentinian served no good purpose, and that the Spanish words most widely accepted suited him best. Whilst eschewing the un-American nightingales of Lugones' generation, he made no efforts to investigate the ornithology of the pampas, a task that had already been adequately undertaken by the Anglo-Argentinian writer W. H. Hudson. But the setting of almost all Borges' stories is in fact Argentinian. Even when the background is allegedly English or European, the most recognizable features of the landscape generally suggest the streets of Buenos Aires or the *quintas*—colonial houses in the suburbs—which stand in large gardens.

In the *Inquisiciones* made between 1925 and 1928 Borges was able to define his own attitude to the literary *avant-garde* of *Martín Fierro*, with whom he now parted company. But more importantly, he clarified his own metaphysical standpoint and developed his brief style, free of excessive adjectives and of avoidable transitional passages. Indeed the style of many of his essays, and afterwards of many of his stories, is surprisingly abrupt.

Until the end of the Twenties, Borges continued to think of himself as a poet, though in one poem of *Luna de enfrente*, 'La vida entera' ('The whole of my life'), he wrote that he expected neither to see nor to make anything new. In fact, however, a group of later poems, published under the title *Cuaderno San Martín* (*The San Martín Exercise Book*) contains the best of his *vers-libre* writing. Indeed one at least of them now bears the mark of his continued approval. If he could discard the rest he would still preserve 'El noche que en el Sur, lo velaron' ('Death watch on the South side'). The poem appears as the sole representative of his early poetry in the *Second Personal Anthology* selected by the poet himself in 1968. He has made only a few small changes in the original text. But the *Cuaderno*—its title merely refers to an exercise book with the Liberator's figure on the cover in which Borges happened to collect the poems—contains one or two other pieces that equally deserve the poet's continued approval: 'Paseo de Julio', a second piece on the cemetery of 'La Recoleta', the baroque 'Fundición mítica de Buenos Aires' ('Mythical foundation of Buenos Aires') and 'Elegia de los portones' ('Elegy of the arches'). In these also he has transcended the Ultraist techniques of which he now so much disapproved. The poems are more objective. 'Elegia de los portones' evokes the Palermo of rattling carts, the fig tree stretching over a gate, and again the pink houses at the corner of an unknown street. It is an elegy, as is also the second poem on La Recoleta, which reviews the ancestral past, now resumed in the living poet, who confronts the problem of death and finds no answer.

The poem on the watching over the dead man has a greater intensity than either of these more elegiac pieces. The circumstances are crisply delineated: the invitation from someone, a name to which he can now attach no face, himself sitting with strangers beside the corpse drinking *maté*, the room leading off a courtyard, the dead man beneath the flowers. The poet asks himself questions which, as in the cemetery poem, have no answers. The dead man is absent; no belief about him is credible. Yet he has given the watchers a certain experience, a release

29

from the 'prolixity or endless round of the real', a taste of an unreality more intense than the dead presence of the corpse.

> And his hospitality in death will give us
> one more memory for time
> and skeletal streets on the South side gradually to be
> gained
> and a dark breeze on my brow as I walk home
> and night that frees us from our greatest torture,
> the endless round of reality.

The dead man can confer his gift of vision and reality because he now partakes of unreality; and when the mourners come out of the death room something strange happens to them.

> (The death watch ravages our faces;
> our eyes are dying up there like Jesus).

This Ultraist extravagance has been allowed to remain in the latest versions of the poem. The unknown mourners have taken part in a communion, and depart, having shared a 'privilege'. 'All privileges, however dark', says the poet, 'belong to the lineage of miracle'.

If this poem touches on unreality and miracle, the equally direct 'Paseo de Julio' conveys a nightmare vision of common reality and lack of communication. Paseo de Julio, the night town of Buenos Aires, with its blaring music, distorting mirrors and glaring brothels is 'the heaven of those in hell, since it lacks the saving unreality of the dead man on the bier'. Borges contrasts the terrible innocence—which is emptiness—of that night town's resignation, of its dawn, of its knowledge, of its unpurified spirit, with the Eden-innocence of his own Palermo where

> Behind the thick walls of my suburb the stout carts
> will pray with raised shafts to their impossible god of
> iron and dust.
> But what god, what idol, what worship are yours,
> Paseo de Julio?
> Your life is death's ally.
> All happiness by its mere existence is opposed to you.

'Paseo de Julio' is a nightmare poem of obsessive 'reality', and one is left with the feeling that the carts with their upturned shafts are only playing at communion, that they have no god out in Palermo capable of purging the hell of the Paseo. The poem is powerful, and ultimately pessimistic. It marks the end of the poet's first creative stage which, beginning in Ultraism, attained a philosophical consequence which Borges now wished to work out in prose. *Cuaderno de San Martín* was awarded second prize in the annual competition promoted by the city of Buenos Aires. The winner of the first prize was a nonentity. Borges would have preferred to receive no award at all. Perhaps this insulting second place strengthened his resolve to give up poetry; at all events he did so.

The late Twenties and early Thirties found Borges writing literary articles for various periodicals and making an occasional anthology or translation. In 1931 he took part in the foundation of the magazine *Sur*, a substantial periodical edited and sustained by an enthusiastic woman of letters, Victoria Ocampo, and supported by the best of the established writers of Argentina. The aim of *Sur* was to present the best of contemporary writing, and it printed work by André Gide, Aldous Huxley, Alberto Moravia, André Malraux; indeed all the leading writers of the day. Borges had now a place. For many of the essays in *Discusion* (1932), the first of his collections to remain in his good graces, were first printed in *Sur*.

The foundation of *Sur* marked Borges' final severance from the *avant-garde*, the generation of *Martín Fierro*, from which he had increasingly differed since his abandonment of Ultraism. Towards the end of the Thirties, moreover, the *Martín Fierro* group was breaking into factions. Some under the prevailing Marxist influences wanted the journal to adopt a political platform; others protested that *Martín Fierro* was neither of the right, the left nor the centre. Neutralism on the whole won the day, and the generation that succeeded was rather surrealist than political. But by this time Borges had passed over to the literary establishment of *Sur*. *Sur* did not open its pages to experiment. Such new writers as it accepted were at least moderate traditionalists, and Borges soon found himself attacked as a conservative by young men who actually shared his admiration for Macedonio Fernández. To the young men, *Sur* appeared from the start to be run by a clique and to be more concerned with foreign values than with Argentinian.

The *Sur* clique was centred on the Ocampo mansion or *quinta* at San Isidro, a small colonial town a few stations further along the line from Palermo. There was Victoria herself, a woman of infinite drive and enthusiasm; her sister Silvina, a poet and afterwards the wife of Adolfo Bioy Casares, a writer of fiction later to be Borges' collaborator in several pseudonymous works; Borges himself; his sister Norah and her husband Guillermo de Torre, a literary theorist who had participated in all the *avant-garde* movements from Dada onwards and had now reached a conservative standpoint; and Eduardo Mallea, a novelist of the Argentine scene, concerned rather with the landowners up-country than with the people of the city.

In 1930 Borges published what had been intended as a biographical and critical study of the poet Evaristo Carriego. Carriego (1883–1912) was a poet in the popular vein who, coming up from the provinces, happened to settle in the suburb of Palermo, where he died when Borges was only thirteen. Carriego had been an acquaintance of Jorge Luis' parents, and had inscribed to them a copy of his single published book which their son had read in Geneva. But when he told them of his plan to write Carriego's life, they tried to dissuade him, observing correctly that he was not a good poet. But for Jorge Luis he represented the life outside his childhood garden and outside the library of the paternal mansion to which the child was confined. There lay the wild Palermo of strong arm gangs, knife-fights and argumentative talk in the cafés and bars. Of this life, Carriego was a spectator, almost a participant. His one or two successful poems were narratives of local manners; the best is 'The Wedding' ('El casamiento'), a pleasantly humorous piece. Another, on the soul of the suburb ('El alma del suburbio') opens to the tune of barrel-organs and the crying of an evening paper. Fifty years later, in the preface to the volume *Evaristo Carriego* in his collected edition, Borges still claimed to see this suburban poet as a precursor, but of what it is hard to say. Borges goes so far as to compare Carriego with Rudyard Kipling, as a representative of the half-breed. It appears that

Carriego had Indian blood, and Borges postulates some Eurasian admixture in Kipling.

Carriego's raw romantic outbursts and his ironical popular narratives are more commonplace than Borges will admit. Their interest indeed is purely local and their chief merit is that they provided Borges with the opportunity to write about the life, as he imagined it, outside the garden walls. To quote an early poem of Stephen Spender, bewailing a similar confinement, Borges' parents kept him 'from children who were rough'. Evaristo Carriego is an imaginative and idealising study of these very rough children and their murderous parents.

Carriego was bitter, unsuccessful and tubercular. He was steeped in the local life, admired and drank with the bullies, thieves and murderers; and this gave Borges his opportunity for writing a book, not on the dead poet, who was the merest excuse, but on the history and customs of Palermo and its exemplary importance for Argentina itself. The history of Palermo was for Borges the history of the country. He began his book with an essay on Palermo as the site of a battle against Rosas, of its first houses, its unpaved streets and, of course, of the inhabitants of its shacks and their fights. For a few pages, indeed, it seems that the central character of the book will be, not the tubercular poet but a certain Murana, possibly the hero of Carriego's poem 'El guapo' ('The ruffian'), who at the turn of the century performed murders on commission, neither boasting of them nor concealing them. This sets Borges theorising on the Argentinian's natural sympathy for the criminal, not the police: a characteristic which he shares with the Spaniard. The killing of a guitarist, a murderous knife-battle after a challenge between strangers, the tale of a ghost swinging from a lamp-post, give Borges opportunities for condensed narrative which show the way in which he was developing towards the short story. But at the same time, an account of the etymology and conventions of 'el truco', a card game corresponding to the American 'brag', is only one of several disquisitions for which Carriego provides a thin excuse. Not only the etymology of 'el truco' but the history of the tango and its lyric, the *milonga*, take Borges away from his ostensible subject. He believes that the tango originated in the brothels of Buenos Aires, and argues strongly against rival theories. Another essay on the mottoes painted on old carts, which Borges saw as a kind of folk-poetry, finds an uneasy home in this biographical and literary study.

'I affirm—with no squeamish fear and no new-fangled love of paradox—that only new countries have a past, that is to say an autobiographical memory of it. If time is succession, we must recognise that where the density of events is greatest most time runs, and that the most abundant flow is on this unconscious side of the world.' The opening paradox—for paradox it is despite Borges' denial—might be interpreted as a mere claim that in the new countries more changes have taken place within living memory than in the old, that Palermo has altered more in Borges' memory than a London or Parisian suburb in the same time. But the argument with which Borges attempts to sustain his paradox is more difficult to interpret except as special pleading. The most striking characteristic of Buenos Aires to a stranger is that it has no history, that it is an imitaion Paris set down on the frontier between the flat and shallow expanses of the Plate estuary and the boundless flatness of the pampa. Borges, by reference to local customs and rivalries, was attempting to give the country a past of a local kind. Victoria Ocampo in *Sur* sought in an opposite sense to graft into a weak native stock a sliver from the great tree of the European literary tradition. These two seemingly contrary endeavours were present in Borges' contributions to the magazine.

When pressed by interviewers to confess to the personal psychological basis of his best stories, Borges frequently objects that they are not subjective at all, but mere half-humorous inventions, a series of playful elaborations of philosophical ideas. This explanation of the stories is offered, perhaps, only to interviewers who seem particularly bent on eliciting private confessions. Generally Borges is content to allow the personal element in the stories without being specific about it. The essays in *Discusión* (1932) can for the most part be described as playful elaborations on philosophical or theological themes. In the preface of 1952 Borges confesses to his 'incredulous but perpetual affection for theological difficulties.' His exposition of the gnostic theories of Basilides, his disquisition on the Kabbalah, and his speculation on 'the duration of hell' coolly set out, with the apparent impartiality of a Montaigne, the various absurd arguments of writers in the obscure past. He is most deeply engaged when his subject breaks the bounds of reason to create a sublime mountain of unreason, which is in fact a myth. The incredulous Borges draws back half-believing. Magic is for him perpetually compelling. One essay on 'The narrative art and magic' contrasts stories full of hints and portents with the mere psychological realism of the conventional novel. Psychology or character is for him less important than myth or creation. The real Whitman was a drab little man; the 'other Whitman' who gives his name to the essay, was a hero of the poet's own creation.

Discusión, and the subsequent essays contributed to *Sur* and not yet collected in book form, explore and attempt paradoxes of credulity only to draw back. One is reminded of Macdedonio's resolve to believe in nothing in order to have nothing to lose at death. But the essays of *Discusión*, even the more trivial ones, testify to a search for something—if not for an ultimate truth, at least for a firm ground of rejection. He had renounced poetry, and *Evaristo Carriego* had proved to him that the study of a man was not his form of expression. He afterwards reflected that perhaps the fault lay in the subject, that he might have written more successfully of Macedonio or Lugones. But in fact his concern was with books, not men. In books he could find, perhaps, a credible myth. Berkeley and Schopenhauer were important to him, not as philosophers to be studied, but as the inventors of possibly valid explanations of the world and its 'theological difficulties'.

4   Towards a Crisis

In the six years following the foundation of *Sur*, Borges continued
to write essays for that periodical and notices of books for the
literary supplements of two newspapers and also for the publishing house run by *Sur*. He translated two books by Virginia Woolf,
Orlando and *A Room of One's Own*. *Historia universal de la infamia*
('The Universal History of Infamy' 1935), his next book, is a ten-
tative essay in myth-making. Already in *Discusión* he had been
speculating on methods of narration, on the introduction of
magic into fiction. But his first necessity was to tell a story, and to
lend it significance. The title of the book shows its intention: its
subject was crime considered mythically as a recurring theme.
No longer was he concerned primarily with Argentina, though the
book's one original story 'Hombre de la esquina rosada' ('The
Man at the Pink Corner') reverts to Palermo and could as well
have been appended to *Evaristo Carriego* as to this book. The
universality of the theme also goes back to the poet's Palermo
childhood. For the stories are recastings, in a manner which
Borges claims to have learnt from Stevenson and Chesterton, of
stories taken from English books, stories of pirates, of gangsters, of
slave-dealers, indeed of the whole gamut of crime or infamy.
These stories are flatly told, varying from the originals from
which they were taken only in the interests of a mythlike simplicity. They are not very interesting in themselves. Their merit
rather lies in Borges' assemblage of this particular group as
universal representatives of infamy.

'The Man at the Pink Corner' is an entirely successful invention, embodying in a sordid tale of a suburban knifing that element of magic in the form of mystification that Borges demanded
of a narrative. The story has been adapted both as film and ballet.
It was from the start a kind of spoken ballet of formal gestures—a
challenge, a refusal to fight, a woman's transfer of loyalty from the

apparent coward to the challenger, a murder, a muttered confession by the murderer. 'All is sheer choreography! The movements are hieratic. There is no motivation, no psychology.' Borges once said that if he could catch the speech of a character, then he had caught the character. The people of this story speak a kind of formalised Argentinian. Borges says that the story was written as a memorial to an old ruffian whose tales of past violence delighted him. He wanted to catch the ring of this man's voice. The story took him many months to write and, when finished, it was printed with the other tales of *The Universal History of Infamy* in the literary pages of the evening paper to which Borges contributed, where they aroused no particular notice. No doubt the average reader regarded them as mere filling-in matter, the retelling of old crime stories that could be trumped any night by the real happenings in Buenos Aires streets. For Borges, they were a valuable first exercise in the art of narrative.

Having established his powers of writing adventure in the plain prose of Stevenson's *Treasure Island* or Chesterton's Father Brown stories, Borges moved on to consider in the essays of his next collection, *Historia de la eternidad* (*History of Eternity* 1936), certain permanent questions of literary technique and certain fundamental 'theological difficulties'. The overall impression is of a writer feeling his way forward from mere inventiveness to a solid and traditional style, and at the same time of a philosophical adventurer, poised on the Pascalian knife-edge between absolute faith and absolute despair, seeking a reasonable ground for at least a qualified optimism. The first preoccupation is the subject of two essays on metaphor and a pendant consideration of three translations of the *Arabian Nights* into English and French.

Dealing with metaphor, Borges rejects by implication the practices of Ultraism, touching rather on the use of the metaphor as an object in itself by Góngora and Quevedo. Góngora's unfinished masterpiece 'Las soledades' has the most tenuous story, he notes elsewhere; it is nothing but a pretext for metaphorical elaboration. On the other hand, in early Norse poetry the metaphors or *kennigar* are a mere cold substitution of an analogy for an object: for 'the air' they write 'the home of the winds', for a battle 'a feast of eagles' or a 'rain of red shields'. . . . Borges makes a lengthy catalogue of these *kennigar*, listing their use singly or combined to

37

make what is almost a code language. In later literature, he rebukes the seventeenth century writer Gracian, and among more modern writers, Baudelaire and Lugones, for a similar repetitive frigidity. Borges' conclusion is that between the two extremes of arbitrary and stereotyped metaphor can be found a middle course, the refurbishment of the *topoi* or commonplaces, such as the comparison of women with flowers that is to be found in poetry from the *Song of Solomon* onwards. It is along these lines that Borges himself worked when he returned to the writing of poetry in the Sixties. Deliberately, he returned to stock themes, to traditional treatments and metaphors, giving them the new look that he had postulated twenty-five years before in these essays. By then his standpoint was definitely conservative. But in a footnote to his essay on the *kenningar* he acknowledged that his own loyalties were divided. Indeed in his loving catalogue of the old Icelandic baroquisms, he showed that such a code language was still attractive to him.

The essays in *Discusión* were spattered with quotations, and references to early and obscure writers, and even richer in testimonies to his wide reading are the pages, footnotes and appended lists of authorities in the *History of Eternity*. It is as if Borges were playing a game of scholarship, constructing his essays from the pickings of other men's thoughts as he had constructed the stories of his *Universal History of Infamy* from borrowings of twice-told tales.

Behind such a façade of quotation and ascription, Borges attempted in the title essay of the *History of Eternity* and two smaller essays on time and eternity to conceal the existential anxiety which compelled him to seek a small platform of ironic certainty in the shifting waters of cosmological speculation. In several of the early poems, Borges had recorded moments of self-awareness associated with repeated sunsets that were in fact one eternal sunset of his childhood, and with a certain sense of waking to the reality of his real self in the course of night walks through the suburbs of Buenos Aires. The memory of these moments called vividly to his mind the recurrent pink street corner and the unexpected view of the pampa in the dawn at the end of a road. They were associated with a sensation of *déjà vu*, that he had been here before. These experiences gave him the taste of eternity.

In ancient cosmologies these experiences were connected with two concepts concerning time and its transcendence. In his first essay, Borges considered various theories of eternity. Rejecting the complete transcendetalism of Plotinus, by reference to the Platonic doctrine of ideas, Borges explained his own nostalgia for the one sunset that lay behind all the appearances of sunset. But eternity is inconceivable, he demurs, rejecting his short-lived Platonic acceptance. Yet time is equally inconceivable. The essay ends on the note of almost-belief: 'Life is too poor not to be immortal.' The two other metaphysical essays are attempts to dispel a nightmare, the fear of Eternal recurrence: an endless repetition of the same life, almost unaltered, one life only divided from the next by the short interval of death. Borges does not confess that this is his own nightmare, nor refer here—though he does in a later poem—to himself suffering from insomnia. But he quotes Richard Burton's attribution of Nietzsche's preoccupation with this idea to his suffering from 'the crucifixion of a sleeplessness.' Borges refutes the idea mathematically, by an argument based on the action of entropy and on the very literal question: 'Who or what is it that prevents the many lives from coalescing?' He quotes Heraclitus, Nietzsche, P. D. Ouspensky and, without attributing the argument to the last-named Russian philosopher, decides that the only escape from recurrence is to realise that you are living in it. At such moments, Borges concludes, a man becomes aware of his own destiny. But these moments are akin to those of *déjà vu*, which can be explained by a mechanical trick of the perceptions whereby an impression is recorded before it is perceived. Borges' escape from his nightmare of recurrence appears to be only partial.

A complete escape is however suggested by the story 'El aceramiento de Almutasim' ('The Approach to Almutasim'), which is included in the volume. It is one of the most ingenious that Borges has written. It appears as one of two notes, the second on 'the Art of Abuse' being of minor importance. Both are disguised as book notices. 'The Approach to Almutasim' purports to give an account of a novel by an Indian lawyer first published in Bombay (1952) and subsequently in a revised form by Victor Gollancz in London with an introduction by Dorothy Sayers. This last name would suggest that the book was a detective story.

Actually, from the two principal scenes which Borges relates, it was a novel of search. In the opening scene, a young man believes that he has killed a demonstrator in a brawl between Hindus and Muslims and, taking refuge in a tower, climbs to the top where he finds a sordid individual who tells him that he lives by robbing corpses. He goes on to describe certain loathsome horse-thieves. The young man goes to sleep, and when he wakes the old man has gone. But the thought of those horse thieves remains in his mind. He realises that the robber of corpses has presented him with a compulsive clue—a Zahir, it is called in a subsequent story. After this first scene, which Borges in his capacity of reviewer compares to a story by Kipling, there follow nineteen chapters of wanderings and adventures, 'among people of the vilest class'. In one of his sordid acquaintances he sees 'the reflection of a friend, or the friend of a friend.' He decides that somewhere in the world there is a person from whom this clarity emanates. This is Almutasim, whom the young man eventually meets as a voice from behind a cheap curtain loaded with beads in the gallery of an obscure bazaar. The voice bids him come in. Has he found the God he was seeking? Borges as commentator retreats into a web of complications. Perhaps the being he has found is himself in search of another Being, and that Being in search of another, ad infinitum. A note, and a note on this note, lead us to a Persian poem, to Spenser's *Faerie Queene*, and to the *Arabian Nights*. But as in the case of the metaphysical essays, one does not find it hard to detect the author's preoccupation, his existential anxiety and his refusal to give due importance to his own intuitional solutions. His scholarship is the smoke-screen of one unwilling or unable to suspend entirely his disbelief.

Jorge Luis Borges was now in his late thirties, unmarried, a leading man of letters in his own country but hardly known outside it, a contributor to various periodicals, yet no more able than any other man of letters in Argentina to live by writing. Dependent on family money, he spent much time at the country hotel of Adrogué, described as Triste-le-Roy in his subsequent story 'La muerte y la brújula' ('Death and the Compass'). Though he read much and his vision was at that time good enough to enable him to write about films, he knew that his eyes were failing, and that he would end, like his father, and his English grandmother and her father before, virtually blind. The hereditary disease had affected him since boyhood. Yet books were his life. Occasionally in the poems appear the figures of somewhat idealised young ladies, a sad suggestion of lost loves, and clearly his relations with his fellow writers, the men and particularly the women, were close. But Borges' inner despair, studiously hidden beneath an impassive exterior, is patently revealed in an isolated poem of 1936, 'Insomnio' ('Insomnia'). Here are all the stable values of *Luna de enfrente* reversed: the suburban street, the pampa, lights, mirrors, foliage are details in recurrent visions of half-sleep. The night must be a cage of curved iron bars not to be broken by the disorderly visions that fill it. The oppression conveyed by this rasping image is unmistakable. But the poem proceeds to even greater depths of horror, to the dread of a hideous immortality:

> Wire, building lots, waste paper, the garbage of
>   Buenos Aires.
> Tonight I believe in a terrible immortality:
> no man has ever died, no woman, no dead person,
> for this inescapable iron and clay reality must violate
> the impassivity of all who are asleep or dead
> —even though they hide in century-long corruption
> and must condemn them to a hideous wakefulness.

This poem equals in horror James Thomson's 'The City of Dreadful Night' or such a poem of Baudelaire as 'Les sept vieillards'. Borges has denied in interviews that he has wished to induce anguish in his readers. Yet he certainly conveys his own anguish, as he admitted in an answer to a question of one of his most pertinacious interviewers, Alex Zisman. Borges has seen a performance by a British actor who read extracts from his works in a frenzied manner before a semicircle of mirrors, running from one large blank book to another. Borges expressed some surprise but no anger at this presentation of his writings. 'It was as if the whole of my past had caved in on top of me' he told Zisman, 'not a very comfortable kind of sensation'. It no doubt carried him back to his feelings of the late Thirties.

In the year of 'Insomnio', Borges' life had in some sense 'caved in'. Moreover Argentina itself had been sliding for five or six years from a brief spell of parliamentary democracy which ended in corruption, by way of various dictatorial interludes, towards the abyss of the Peronist revolution of 1940. Borges clung to the values of the Conservative 'oligarchs', but their leaders were showing themselves no more competent and no less corrupt than their Radical predecessors. Their power was 'caving in' also. The Borges family had been closely united, almost exclusive: the blind English grandmother, the blind father, the mother, a woman of great talent who was responsible not only for them but for her bachelor son, whose sight was already failing. But Fanny Haslam died at the age of eighty in 1935, and her son, the poet's father, in 1938. Borges' relationship with his mother became closer, and shortage of money forced him to take any small permanent job that he could find. He took a post—clearly a semi-sinecure—as cataloguer in one of the city's branch libraries, in a drab suburb. Every day he went to work. But the work was negligible. The inflated staff had agreed among themselves to work at a leisurely pace in order that no one should be sacked as redundant. Borges found his fellow librarians unsympathetic; 'they were interested in nothing but racing, football and dirty stories.' But Borges held this job for about nine years, 'years of solid unhappiness', he commented. But either on the roof in summer, or in the basement in winter, having completed the small number of catalogue entries agreed on among the staff, Borges pursued his own reading and writing, untroubled by his superiors. The job was not exacting, though the salary was small. Yet the sordid surroundings and uncultured company helped to produce the anguish recorded in 'Insomnio', as can be judged from the story 'La Biblioteca de Babel' ('The Library of Babel') in which that library is described, magnified to such infinite dimensions as to be commensurate with the world. That branch of the Municipal Library of Buenos Aires has been eternalised as a nightmare scene by its First Assistant Cataloguer.

On Christmas Eve 1938 Borges met with a seemingly trivial accident. He was mounting the staircase of a block of flats, when owing to his bad sight he stumbled against a tilted window-frame, grazing his head. The wound was slight, but it turned septic. For a week or so he lay sleepless in a high fever. He suffered from hallucinations, and one evening lost the power of speech. He was then rushed to a nursing-home, where an emergency operation was performed. For some days he lingered, unknowingly, between life and death.

Borges' experiences in his illness seem to have followed those recorded in 'Insomnio'. He feared that he had lost his reason, that he would never write again, that he would not be able to understand anything that was read to him. Of his nightmares he later recorded one in the story 'El sur' ('The South') which tells of a man leaving a hospital to recuperate in the south. Arriving at a country station, he goes into the bar, where he is insulted and challenged by a local gangster. The man behind the bar, who watches events impassively, reminds him of one of the attendants at the hospital, and the insulting gangster hits him with a bread pellet on the head, at the place where he had been operated on. Borges' alter ego of the story is knifed and dies. The weapon is one of those very knives that had been for the poet symbols of the tough life outside the protecting walls of his childhood.

As he recovered, Borges' mother read him a novel that had just arrived from England, C. S. Lewis' *Out of the Silent Planet*. Borges burst into tears on finding that he could really understand. But there was a further question: Would he ever write again? To discover the answer, he set himself the task of writing one of the most extraordinary of the tales afterwards collected in *Ficciones*: 'Pierre Mesnard, autor del *Quijote*' ('Pierre Mesnard, Author of the *Quixote*').

In a later essay on 'Partial Magic in *Don Quixote*', Borges argues that the book's magic lies not in its parodies of romantic tales, for *Amadis* was pilloried as a tissue of absurdities, nor yet, as for the present day, in the magic of the countryside, which for a modern reader is enchanted land. For Cervantes' contemporaries the inns and roads of La Mancha were no more magical than a filling-station on one of these roads is for us. The magic, as Borges saw it, lay in the overlapping of planes of reality. As the barber goes through the books in Don Quixote's library, he comes across the *Galatea*, whose author, a certain Miguel de Cervantes, is, he says, a friend of his 'more deeply versed in misfortunes than in verses'. Again, in the second part of the book, Don Quixote and Sancho prove to have read the chronicle of their adventures set out in the first part. 'Every novel' writes Borges 'is an ideal plane inserted into the realm of reality', and in some works, perhaps the greatest, a kind of double insertion takes place; events are mirrored as in a dream within a dream, and the play in *Hamlet* repeats in its rough outline the events of the play itself. However 'the imperfect correspondence of the principal and secondary work reduces the efficacy of its inclusion'. Borges' conclusion leads him to one of the fundamental paradoxes of his metaphysical fantasy. Since 'The inventions of philosophy are no less fantastic than those of art' and, as *Don Quixote* proves, 'the characters of a work of fiction can at the same time be its readers or spectators, we readers or spectators may ourselves be fictitious.'

A sick man, returning to the 'reality' of books and writing, he started to invent a fable which should throw doubt on the relations of truth and fiction by charting an intersection of planes, at which neither is completely the one or the other. The story fills only twelve pages, the first four of which are devoted to establishing the reality of a minor French writer named Pierre Mesnard. His very minor works are listed, his relationships to living authors—to Paul Valéry in particular—touched on, and the ladies who patronised him ironically introduced. At this point Mesnard is real, and Borges appears to be writing not a story but a literary note. He again uses the device of 'The Approach to Al-Mutasim'. But then Mesnard sets out to perform a magical feat: to rewrite *Don Quixote*. It would have been possible by Borges' fantastic reasoning for this provincial Frenchman to return to the temporal position of Cervantes: to become a Catholic, to fight the Moors and the Turks and to forget all European history between 1602 and the moment of his writing. It would have been possible to write a modern *Don Quixote*, to bring the knight into the contemporary world. This is what Unamuno did in his vast extended commentary, the *Vida de Don Quijote y Sancho*. But Mesnard's aim was to write the book afresh in the identical words, as if he himself had conceived it. This is in effect what every reader does when he reads an old work. He reads it with all the centuries' agglomeration of changed viewpoints and historical experiences, by the light of which he is often tempted, as Mesnard was, to expand or alter the text. Cervantes, in Chapter XXXVIII of Part One, comparing the relative merits of the careers of Arms and of Letters, decided for the military virtues, for the life of action. But this in

1938 smacks of 'trahison des clercs', the nascent anti-intellectualism of the intellectual. Yet in 're-writing' this chapter—it was one of the few that he completed—Mesnard in no way varied from the text of his illustrious exemplar. Yet Borges, his fictitious reader, recognised in every phrase the tone of voice of the latter day book's French author. 'The text of Cervantes and that of Mesnard are verbally identical' writes Borges, 'but the second is almost infinitely richer. More ambiguous, his detractors will say, but ambiguity is richness.' The actual *Don Quixote* is also ambiguous, he might have said more plainly, supposing he had seen virtue in plain statement, because it is at the same time a seventeenth century work composed within the intellectual context of its own day, and the work which, like Pierre Mesnard, every contemporary reader invests with the altered values of his own time, yet without changing—for he is powerless to do so—a single word of Cervantes' text.

In testing his own recovered health by this exercise in unresolved ambiguities, Borges entered a field that he was to explore in his two collections of 'fictions', which occupied him for the next ten years—the time of his greatest accomplishment. In attempting a remedial five-finger exercise, he ended by sending to the magazine *Sur* an inverted fugue of unresolved complexities, which is today considered one of his outstanding compositions. Borges himself uttered a wry comment on Pierre Mesnard's laborious reconstruction of Cervantes' text in one of the sketches in *Cronicas de Bustos Domecq* (1967), a kind of *sottiserie* of modern aesthetic eccentricities. The fictitious Bustos Domecq masks the figures of Borges himself and the novelist Adolfo Bioy Casares, who had previously collaborated in the detective stories *Seis problemas para Don Isidro Parodi* (*Six Problems for Don Isidro Parodi* 1942). In the sketch 'Homenaje a César Paladion' ('Homage to César Paladíon'), an elderly Argentinian writer is presented whose habit it was to rewrite in the Mesnard manner all the masterpieces of world literature and who, having completed *Uncle Tom's Cabin*, was engaged when he died on a 'work of a Biblical type' entitled *The Gospel according to Saint Luke*.

Two major stories, which accompany 'Pierre Mesnard' in the first section of *Ficciones* (1956) invent two possible worlds, fictitious alternatives to our own, which enrich the world of 'reality', each

45

in its separate way, with a different kind of ambiguity. These are 'La Biblioterca de Babel' ('The Library of Babel') and 'La loteria de Babilonia ('The Lottery in Babylon'). Each adumbrates a philosophical system; and philosophical systems are, by Borges' description, nothing but poetic hypotheses or works of art. Each at the same time reveals its maker's existential anxiety.

Two predominant symbols recur in Borges' stories, that of refracting mirrors—the many possible versions of *Don Quixote*, for example—and that of the search—as in 'The Approach to Al-Mutasim'—which generally implies a maze or labyrinth from which there may or may not be a way out. 'The Library of Babel' is a maze made from the multiple reduplication of the Municipal Library in which the poet reluctantly worked. As in a nightmare, it is immediately presented as vast, infinite, co-extensive with the whole of experience.

The universe (which others call the Library) is composed of an indefinite and perhaps infinite number of hexagonal galleries, with huge ventilation shafts in the middle, surrounded by very low railings. From every hexagon, the floors below and above are visible interminably. The arrangement of the galleries is invariable. Twenty shelves—five long shelves on each side—cover all the sides but two; their height, which is that of each floor, hardly exceeds that of the average librarian.

The nightmare—a recurrent Piranesi prison—is established in these opening lines; the height of each floor is the height of a man —of the librarian, who is the dreamer himself. In this claustrophobic 'universe' a man may travel from his youth, perhaps in search of a book, perhaps of 'the catalogue of catalogues'. The books are infinite in number and absolutely uniform. Each shelf contains thirty-two books of four hundred and ten pages. Each page contains forty lines of eighty black letters each. Whichever way a librarian may move through the hexagonal maze, he will find no variation. All the books are in cipher, and no one can be certain what the ciphers mean. There is a legend in the library that tells how

> Five hundred years ago the head of one of the upper
> hexagons came across a book as baffling as the rest but
> which contained nearly two pages of homogeneous

lines. He showed this to an ambulant decoder who said
that they were written in Portuguese. Others told him
that they were in Yiddish. In less than a century the
language was established: a Samoyed Lithuanian
dialect of Guarani with classical Arabic inflections.

A sour joke at the expense of classical philosophy. So much as can
be discovered about the nature of the universe in five hundred
years is no more than a jumble of conflicting languages. Yet

> Everything is there: the detailed history of the future;
> the autobiographies of the archangels, the true
> catalogue of the Library and thousands of thousands of
> false catalogues, the proof of the falsity of those
> catalogues, the proof of the falsity of the true catalogue.

And infinitely more. In fact the Library comprised all books and
when the librarians learnt this they were glad, for they 'felt themselves to be masters of a secret, intact treasure', and set out on a
search in all directions.

> In some shelf of some hexagon (men reasoned) there
> must exist a book which is the cipher and perfect
> compendium of all the rest; some librarian has run
> through it and is analogous to a god.

Superstitions, religions, heresies are all hinted at by analogy to the
search and the reading of those books. But there is no certainty;
the librarians live and die in the search, and their bodies are
thrown down the shafts between the hexagons. The dreamer's
conclusion is acutely pessimistic.

> I suspect that the human species—the unique human
> species is about to be extinguished, and the Library
> will endure for ever: lamp-lit, solitary, infinite,
> perfectly immobile, furnished with precious volumes,
> useless, incorruptible, secret.

But perhaps, Borges admits in his final paragraph, the Library
is not 'limitless but cyclical'. 'If an eternal traveller were to cross

it in any direction, he would find after centuries that the same volumes were repeated in the same disorder (which thus repeated would be an order: the Order). My solitude is gladdened by this slight hope.'

This ultimate solution of the problem of infinity conforms to some astronomical speculations. It offers some way out of the nightmare of a recurrent universe, and Borges' dread of this trap was expressed in the essays of the *History of Eternity*. Perhaps in recurrent disorder there is some final order to be discovered.

'The Lottery in Babylon' suggests no final order, only an increasing and ever more baffling disorder, a world disintegrating under the impact of ever more random chance. The people of Babylon invent a lottery, whereby at first only small prizes are distributed. But this lottery becomes popular. More and more people wish to take part, and, for greater excitement, penalties are awarded as well as prizes. Within a few generations the Company, which was believed to administer this lottery, was forced by popular pressure to extend it to the whole of every man's life. Then men began to elaborate theories of chance, as applied to the lottery. Thus a kind of theology or cosmology was established. The teller of the tale observes:

> Under the beneficent influence of the Company our customs have become permeated by chance. The buyer of a dozen jars of Damascus wine will not be surprised if one of them contains a talisman or a viper. The scribe who draws up a contract hardly ever fails to introduce some erroneous detail. I myself, in this hurried report, have falsified some splendour, some atrocity, perhaps also some mysterious monotony.

All is subject to chance. A man is by turns a proconsul, a slave, omnipotent, despised, a prisoner, all according to the chance of the lottery, which is administered by the mysterious and all powerful Company. But what if the Company has never existed and never will? Then Babylon—the Universe—is nothing but an infinite game of chance.

Metaphysical speculations of nightmare intensity rather than stories, for they contain no characters and no action, these establish Borges' method of narration. They are not, like 'The Approach to Al-Mutasim' and 'Pierre Mesnard, Author of the *Quixote*', or the less important 'Investigation of the Writings of Herbert Quain', literary essays with fictitious subjects. Their subject is the Universe as chaos, or rather the Universe as perhaps explicable by the use of a philosophical key which no man has discovered. But the existence of such a key is suggested by the light that seeps from behind Al-Mutasim's curtain. The 'Company' may not exist. Yet a search—life-long, determined, but without hope, self-importance or self-expectation—may lead to a door out of the labyrinth.

5   *Ficciones*

The *Ficciones* did not appear complete until 1945, seven years after the writing of the first story. The intervening years saw the gradual deterioration—seen at least from Borges' point of view—of Argentinian conditions. The oligarchs were losing hold, and a series of ineffective governments were yielding to a popular discontent that was to culminate in Juan Perón's seizure of power in 1946. Throughout the war against Hitler, Borges was an outspoken supporter of the Allies, where many Argentinian politicians, and even intellectuals, were pro-German. Borges returned after his recovery to his post as librarian and continued to work at a number of translations and anthologies as well as at his own tales. Among the authors he translated for the editorial house of *Sur* were Kafka, Faulkner and Henri Michaux. He also compiled two anthologies in collaboration with Adolfo Bioy Casares and his wife Silvina Ocampo. The first, of 'fantastic literature' (1940), contains some pieces that must be attributed to the anthologists themselves, while the second, of Argentinian poetry (1944) is remarkable rather for its exclusions and its timid conservatism than for any great originality. Only Borges' characteristic introduction, with its wayward references to Nietzsche and Samuel Butler and its savage attack on American culture, already quoted, give the book any character. For the rest everyone, from Evaristo Carriego to Silvina Ocampo herself, is represented by one or two poems.

In 1941 Borges submitted as many stories as were so far written for the National Literary Prize, and was passed over. Next year *Sur* published a special number in his honour, deploring the jury's failure to award him the prize. Two years later a new prize sponsored by the Argentinian Society of Authors was founded and the first award made to Borges. Already he and his work were the subject of literary political controversy.

The remainder of the 'fictions' were written slowly. The night-mare element diminishes; artifice or fantasy is more predominant, though at moments the note of horror is insistent. 'Tlön, Uqbar, Orbis Tertius' is the logical working out of a fantasy. Supposing there existed a secret organisation engaged in disseminating knowledge or perhaps merely a fictitious viewpoint that will change the whole of man's activity on earth, how will this organisation proceed? Its first move is to interpolate at the end of a volume of an encyclopedia an article on a hither to unknown mediaeval country in Asia Minor, named Uqbar. The volume is discovered after dinner one night by Borges and Bioy Casares. No other copy of this volume of the encyclopedia contains this article. No clues lead any further; none of the four books listed in the article's bibliography is to be found, though one is mentioned in an old sale list. Then a mysterious traveller called Herbert Ashe, vaguely known to Borges, dies in a Buenos Aires hotel, having received a few days before a package posted in Brazil, which proves to contain an odd volume of the *Encyclopedia of Tlön*, a planet known only to the mysterious people of Uqbar. So far the story concerns only a bibliographical search. The names and opinions of various writers, Argentinian and French, strengthen the credibility of the fantasy. Speculation as to the existence or non-existence of the remaining volumes of Herbert Ashe's encyclopedia leads to a proposal by Borges' Mexican friend Alfonso Reyes that the missing volumes shall be rewritten. But this proves unnecessary. The extant volume describes the languages of Tlön. In the planet's *Ursprache*, the basic unit was the verb; there were no nouns. But in the more developed language of the north,

> The primal unit is not the verb but the monosyllabic adjective. Nouns are formed by the accumulation of adjectives. They do not say 'moon' but 'round airy-light-on-dark' or 'range-faint-of-the-sky', or some other combination.

Thus 'ideal objects abound, evoked and dissolved in a moment according to poetic requirements'. There is no word for moon. The only way in which to describe moonrise over the sea would be: 'Upward above the ever flowing there was mooning.' Every event is consequently individual; there can be no generalisation, no dogma. Their geometry too is different, for they do not relate what they see to what they touch; and the visual system is the more highly valued. Also their books are different from those of our world.

> Books of fiction are based on a single plot with all its imaginable permutations. Works of philosophy invariably include both the thesis and the antithesis . . . a book that does not contain its anti-book is incomplete.

Thus from its linguistic and scientific theories, the whole picture of what may be called our anti-planet is reconstructed. It is monistic, all its beliefs resting on an extreme idealism, by which every event is entirely fresh, in which nothing is learnt from the past, and relativism is all embracing. It is the world of poetic vision, or of mystical identity with the absolute. In it there can be no fixed measure of time or space. As the story ends, the world is becoming influenced by the secret doctrine of Tlön and all the sciences of our planet are in process of reformation. A scattered dynasty of solitary men has changed the face of the world.

And who are the solitary men who have inculcated their poetic idealism, starting from the miracle or the sleight of hand by which an article was inserted in a single copy of an encyclopedia? One thinks of the Mahatmas of Madame Blavatsky, influencing and governing the world from their solitary Himalayan caves. And of the poets, in Shelley's well-worn phrase 'the unacknowledged legislators of the world.' But Borges is merely exploring a hypothesis, rather in the manner of Samuel Butler's *Erewhon* than as a theosophical possibility.

The novels written in Tlön contain a single plot with all its possible permutations. Borges' concern in his fictions is always with plot rather than with characters. 'All the rest is psychology,' he remarked contemptuously in an essay in *Discusión* on the narrative art and magic. Citing *Moby Dick*, a story by Poe and one or two obscure Hollywood films, Borges claims that in a tale of 'manifold vicissitudes' what is most necessary is the magic of certain recurring symbols or motifs that reflect backwards and forwards throughout the narrative. The whiteness of Melville's whale, for example, casts a kind of 'sympathetic magic' on the reader. Borges cites the arguments of Frazer's *Golden Bough*, and one sees its strange relevance for the tale of mystery and imagination, perhaps in the form of scattered clues, perhaps for the detective story in general. Certainly it is relevant to some of Borges' own stories, 'El zahir' ('The Zahir'), 'El Aleph' ('The Aleph') and 'El jardin de senderos que se bifurcan' ('The Garden of Forking Paths'). For in each, the recurrent clue is announced in the story's title.

'The Garden of Forking Paths' is a 'narrative of manifold vicissitudes' all utterly incredible; no Borges story makes it so difficult for the reader even momentarily to suspend disbelief. There is no credible characterisation, and the plot itself wanders down every conceivable fork in the paths of this magical garden, to end in the gratuitous murder of a scholar, an expert in Chinese literature, Doctor Stephen Albert. The garden is fantastic. Yet perversely Borges places it somewhere in the English Midlands in the summer of 1916, at the height of the battle of the Somme. The purpose of the murder by a disillusioned spy of Chinese birth is to prove himself not so much to his German employers as to himself. Albert's name corresponded to that of the town of Albert, from which the British army was to launch its offensive, and the announcement of his murder by the spy in the English newspapers would give the Germans the clue. The spy is hanged 'full of contrition and weariness.' But the central symbol of the story is the garden itself, which Dr Albert and the spy discuss before the perfunctory murder is committed. It is the subject of an obscure Chinese classic, known to them both, the Chinese scholar and the Chinese spy. In fact it contains their own story.

> 'Fang, let us say, has a secret,' reasons Albert, 'a stranger calls at his door. Fang resolves to kill him. Naturally there are several possible outcomes. Fang can kill the intruder, the intruder can kill Fang, both may escape; they may both die, and so on. In the work of Ts'ui Pen all possible results occur, and each one is the point of departure for other forkings. Sometimes the paths of this labyrinth converge, for example, you come

53

> to this house, but in one of those possible pasts you are
> my enemy, in another my friend.'

Then after a further philosophical disquisition, Albert continues to analyse all the possibilities of time:

> 'In the majority of them we do not exist; in some you
> exist but not I, in others I but not you, and in yet
> others both of us. In this present one, which a kindly
> fate has granted me, you have reached my house; on
> another while crossing the garden, you find me dead,
> and in yet another I speak these words, but am an
> error, a phantom.'

Thus the mysterious book they are discussing contains them, and all the possible outcomes of their meeting. Compared with this event the 'reality' of espionage and the Somme battle is nothing.

It is not strange that this story, which was the title story of the collection submitted by Borges for the National Literary Prize, did not find favour with the jury. Its jumbled elements of time-relativism, crime, pursuit and symbolism are not so well coordinated as in the other 'fictions', and the outcome is deliberately arbitrary. It is impossible, despite Borges' statement in his essay, to set out all possibilities without deciding in favour of one, and this one is brusquely imposed in order to end the tale. 'Investigation of the Writings of Herbert Quain' ('Examen de la obra de Herbert Quain') is the study of another of Borges' literary figures, a failure, who after writing one passable detective story entitled characteristically *The God of the Labyrinth*, becomes trapped by a theory the reverse of that of 'The Garden of Forking Paths'. He elaborates a theory of the many possible causes leading to each event. His lack of success finally leads him to argue that readers are an extinct species. But out of one of Quain's most frustrating failures, Borges claims to have extracted the plot of his own story now to be considered, 'The Circular Ruins' ('Las ruinas circulares').

Out of the labyrinthine garden, the labyrinthine library, the confused lottery of random chances, there would seem to be no escape. The paths and galleries and possible chances are unending; the poet is the prisoner of temporal of spatial recurrence. But in the 'Approach to Al-Mutasim', written before his illness, there had been a promise of escape, and again in 'The Circular Ruins', the series of inevitable happenings seems to offer a hope of transcendence.

The story of 'The Circular Ruins' is modelled on some tribal creation myth recorded by an anthropologist from an island in the Southern Seas. A man came in a canoe to a lonely island and climbed to the ruined circular temple, in which stood a stone god carved in the shape of a horse or a tiger. Its name was Fire. He lay down to sleep, and was awakened by the sun, now high in the sky. His purpose was to sleep, and deliberately by force of will to dream. He wished by his dream to create a man. He dreamt of many students and finally dismissed them all, keeping back only one 'whose sharp features repeated the dreamer's.' After a while he awoke and realised that he had not dreamed. In a state of lucidity or insomnia he knew that the experiment had failed. He began again, dreaming his man into existence limb by limb, hair by hair, but he lacked life. The man—or magician—appealed to the Fire god who told him to send his 'son' to another temple where he could worship him, the god. Only the magician and the god will know that he is a phantom. The magician wiped out the 'son's' memory and sent him to the other temple. The circular ruins were then destroyed by fire, as they had been many centuries before, and the story ends on this ambiguous note:

> In a birdless dawn, the magician saw the circle of fire licking the walls. For a moment he thought of taking refuge in the water, but then he understood that death was coming to crown his old age and release him from his labours. He walked towards the tongues of flame. But they did not bite into his flesh. They caressed him, they permeated him without heat or combustion. With relief and terror, he realised that he too was a phantom, that another was dreaming him.

One cannot give the myth one single meaning. In the creative process the magician cannot dream up his 'son'; not until he has surrendered him to the god does he become alive. Even so he is a phantom, but this is known only to the magician and to the god. The magician can only create by surrendering his ownership of his creation. Thus far Borges might be speaking of a poem, but the destruction of the temple and the magician's final surrender—his realisation that he too is the dream of some other dreamer—hints at a religious, even mystical significance. The relative world is the dream of a god, who is himself a dream of Brahma, who dwells on a plane above all gods. The influence of the Hindu scriptures, well known to Borges in translation, seems very probable. But the form of the tale suggests rather, as has been said, a creation-myth. What separates 'The Circular Ruins' from all the other 'fictions' except 'The Approach to Al-Mutasim' is its mood of acceptance, even acceptance of the circular or recurrent form of the ruins themselves, and of their repeated existence and destruction. Recurrence itself is tolerable to the poet in this form which suggests the alternate world cycles of creation and destruction of the Hindus, symbolised by the inward and outward breath of Brahma. It would be an exaggeration, however, to describe 'The Circular Ruins',—or the later 'La escritura del dios' ('The God's Script')—as to any degree religious affirmations. At most, they suggest that 'He who will save his life, must lose it' is an arguable hypothesis.

'Artificios', the second section of *Ficciones*, dated 1944 and including two or three undated pieces that may have been written a year or two later, would appear to be subsequent to the 'fictions' themselves. 'The South' however, the story of the murder of the poet's 'other self' in the canteen of a local station, and 'Funes el memorioso' ('Funes the Memorious') seem to belong to the period of nightmare and insomnia that followed Borges' illness. In conversation with Zisman, the poet agreed that 'Funes' was associated with his bouts of insomnia, and that once he had written it, his insomnia ceased. Funes is a Uruguayan peasant in a remote village who suffers from the inability to forget anything. Ever since a tile fell on his head in a storm, his mind has been congested with every detail about everything. He has also strange abilities: he can tell the time without glancing up at the sun, and he can learn foreign languages—English, French, Portuguese and Latin—without effort. Yet he is incapable of thought. For thought requires the forgetting of differences, the power of generalisation, and of this Funes is incapable. His life consequently is a kind of lucid horror, like that of the magician waking in the ruins and knowing that he had not created his dream. Funes' mind is like that of the insomniac to whom everything occurs with hallucinatory intensity and in linear time. But such full knowledge produces only congestion unless Time can have a stop. Time stopped for Funes with his merciful death. But a stop in time for Jaromir Hladik, the Czech poet of 'El milagro secreto' ('The Secret Miracle') facing a Nazi firing squad, brings fulfilment. In the infinitely extended seconds between the sergeant's order to fire and the striking of the bullet, Hladik lives the year that he has needed to finish his play *The Enemies* and thus justify his existence. The story would be a simple time fantasy of the kind written by H. G. Wells, or might even recall the René Clair film in which some scientists at the top of the Eiffel Tower put all Paris to sleep, were it not for Jaromir's introductory dream of a chess-game protracted through generations, which is interrupted by the entry of the Germans into Prague and Jaromir's arrest. Thus the Wellsian time fantasy is extended into the past and future; Jaromir is perhaps a player, perhaps a piece on the board. Perhaps his execution, his intercalated year, his death, are alike a dream.

A similar ambiguity pervades 'Tema del traidor y del heroe' ('Theme of the Traitor and the Hero') in which a hero of the cause of Ireland is discovered by his comrades to be in fact a traitor. But because of his great popularity it is not possible to condemn and execute him. Therefore, with his connivance, an assassination is arranged. A dramatic text is composed and the traitor, who had once translated *Julius Caesar* into Gaelic, acts out all the stages of his entry into Dublin, his speeches, consultations and final appearance in a theatre box, with such perfection that he often improves on the text provided for him. There in the theatre box he is duly assassinated in a manner suggesting the killing of Abraham Lincoln. But in thus taking over the drama of his own death was the traitor perhaps truly the hero that his admirers ever afterwards thought him to be? Borges begins by acknowledging 'the notorious influence of Chesterton'. But the story contains more than the Chestertonian measure of paradox. From the moment of his entry into Dublin the traitor begins to recall not the hero but the Saviour. Can Judas become Jesus? Are they in fact one, the head and tail of the same coin? This is only hinted in this story, but plainly declared in 'Tres versiones de Judas' ('Three Versions of Judas') in which an obscure historian of heresies puts forth the theory that Judas, far from being a traitor, is a hero. For in betraying Jesus, and thus enabling him to die for mankind, Judas incurs his own damnation. But by such a sacrifice, he and not Jesus becomes the Redeemer; and by discovering and revealing this ultimate truth, the obscure historian of heresies realises that he has discovered the 'secret name of God', and by revealing it he takes upon himself the double role of traitor and redeemer. As for the discoverer of this profound truth, 'he died of heart failure on March 1, 1912. Heresiologists will no doubt remember him; he added to the concept of the Son, which seemed exhausted, the complexities of evil and disaster.' Thus Borges abjures his theological complexities, neatly replacing them among the figments of his paradoxical fantasy.

Two other stories, 'El fin' ('The End') and 'La forma de la espada' ('The Shape of the Sword'), might almost pass for 'realistic', did we not know of Borges' contempt for simple narration, and were it not also for a metaphysical transference of personality in both. 'The End', a brief pendant to the gaucho poem 'Martín Fierro' tells how the negro, after the conclusion of Hernández's narrative, killed Martín in a knife fight, and as he departed in some sense assumed the being of the man he had killed. 'His executioner's task completed, he was now nobody. Or rather, he was the other; he had no destiny on earth, and he had killed a man.' There is a hint here, not only that he had assumed Martín's being, but that the act of killing had been a selfless deed in the spirit of the Lord Krishna's council to Arjuna in the *Bhagavadgita*. He had no further destiny; his role was accomplished. The transfer of personality in 'The Shape of the Sword' is also selfless. An Irish immigrant tells the story of his betrayal during the troubles of the Twenties by a man whom he considered his friend. The narrator, whose face is disfigured by the scar of a sword cut, speaks as if he were the betrayed man. But his story becomes confused; the betrayed man was executed. The betrayer received his Judas money and left for Brazil. The man with the scar is the betrayer. The narrator finally explains that he has told his story this way only so that Borges may listen to him to the end. Otherwise he would be disgusted by his cowardice and treachery. But there is in fact more than a hint of a metaphysical identity between betrayer and betrayed, in the sense of Emerson's poem 'Brahma', just as the negro and Martín Fierro become one in the knife duel.

While it is possible to read hidden significances into all Borges' stories, none presents more possible meanings than 'La secta de fénix' ('The Sect of the Phoenix'), and none so successfully baffles a simple explanation. The secret of the sect is age-old, is commonplace, is rather disgusting, is not revealed to children, is embarrassing, uncomfortable, and not alluded to in public. The sect is, like the Sufi of the Moslem world, widespread and anonymous. The story takes the form of a historical note, like those in Borges' books of essays. It suggests an explanation, but all proposed solutions are implausible. Is it the act of sex, which fulfils most of the conditions? Some commentators believe this. But such a crude trick on the reader is not credible in Borges. Has it something to do with the writing of poems, conceived as a somewhat contemptible occupation in the uncultured society of Argentina? It is simpler to conclude that, as with the Sufic, or the Gnostic cults the secret remains a secret. If there were a simple translation of an allegorical or symbolic statement, the statement would lose all poetic value. So a secret that can be explained by a word, a phrase, cannot survive for centuries as the secret of a cult. Its meaning lies in its secrecy.

The majority of Borges' 'Artifices' are short and hinge on a single metaphysical identity or ambiguity. Its most complex piece, 'La Muerte y la brújula' ('Death and the Compass') is more elaborate, comprising four scenes, one for each point of the compass, and suggesting, like 'The Man at the Pink Corner' but unlike any of the later stories, the scenes or movements of a ballet. The setting is Buenos Aires, though the names of the streets and districts are those of some French town. But Borges has not bothered to substantiate his foreign setting. The Rue de Toulon of the story is clearly the night town of Buenos Aires, the Paseo de Julio of his poem. The deserted nineteenth-century mansion in its over-grown park where the climax of the story takes place is, by Borges' free admission, the hotel Adrogué outside the city where he had spent much leisure time.

'Death and the Compass' differs from the other stories in *Ficciones* by its psychological kernel and by the closeness of its plot to that of a conventional thriller. The pursuer, an amateur detective, is himself pursued and eventually murdered by the criminals. While he believes that he understands them, they in fact have such a perfect knowledge of his character and the quirks of his mind that they are able to plan a series of cryptic clues which will certainly tempt him to his doom. From a realistic standpoint, one may ask why they do not kill him at the outset. But had they done so they would have cut short an inevitable process. Lönnrot, the detective, prides himself on being 'pure reason'. He does not solve the mystery of the bloody events at the four points of the compass, the last of which kills him. But he reads the clues, plots the map, and knows where the next blow may be expected. The first murder, in the Hôtel du Nord, is of an obscure rabbi who has come to attend a Talmudic congress. A number of kabbalistic books are found in the rabbi's cupboard, and in his typewriter a paper bearing the words, 'The first letter of the Name has been uttered.' Lönnrot shares his creator's interest in the Kabbalah, and recognises in 'the Name' the secret name of God. The second murder takes place a calendar month later in a western suburb. The victim is one of those tough suburban gansters of whom Borges wrote in *Evaristo Carriego*. On the wall beside the body are scrawled the words, 'The second letter of the Name has been uttered.' Exactly a calendar month later a telephone call to the police from a low rooming house in the Rue de Toulon offers information about the previous two murders. When the police arrive they find that their caller has apparently been abducted. On the wall is scrawled an announcement that the third letter of the Name has been uttered, and in the vanished man's room is found a kabbalistic book in Latin, with a passage underlined to the effect that the Jewish day runs from sunset to sunset. Lönnrot understands the purport of this message and of a further message sent to the police, announcing a fourth murder for the following month and enclosing a map of the city torn from a Baedeker. Lönnrot plots the places of the three previous crimes on the street map, finds them to be equidistant at three points of the compass, makes the necessary measurements and decides that the fourth crime will take place at the mansion of Triste-le-Roy, and that the time will be sunset. The pace of the story then slackens. Lönnrot takes the suburban railway on the expected afternoon, enters the overgrown garden, walks through the empty rooms of the mansion which proves to be a labyrinth, meets the man, Scharlach, who is expecting him. Lönnrot asks him if he is seeking the syllables of the secret Name, and Scharlach answers no. He is seeking something far more ephemeral, the man Erik Lönnrot, who three years before had sent his brother to jail. Slowly the two men discuss the successive stages in the plot which has brought Lönnrot that evening to the labyrinthine mansion and then at the due moment Schlarach shoots Lönnrot dead.

The story should be a pure Chestertonian fantasy were it not for the strange conversation with which it ends.

'In your labyrinth there are three lines too many,' said Lönnrot at last. 'I know of the Greek labyrinth that is a single straight line. So many philosophers have lost themselves on that line that a mere detective may well lose his way. When in some other incarnation you pursue me, Scharlach, pretend to commit (or do commit) a crime at A, a second at B, eight kilometres away, then a third at C, four kilometres from A and B and halfway between them. Then wait for me afterwards at D, two kilometres from A and again half way between them. Kill me at D, as you are going to kill me at Triste-le-Roy'.

'The next time I kill you,' replied Scharlach, 'I promise you that labyrinth consisting of a single line that is invisible and never ends.'

He stepped back a few paces. Then very carefully he fired.

Lönnrot was indeed 'pure reason', and by reason he went to his death, planning as he died, by exercise of an even more rigorous reason, a death to end his next life. The references to the Kabbalah, which seemed purely decorative, a means of striking Lönnrot through his rare intellectual interests, prove in the end to be the heart of the story. Lönnrot's death, with its two preliminary sacrifices, its carnival in the Rue de Toulon and its final neat end is a mystical process, a killing of a minotaur in a labyrinth and a ' deed that takes place in recurrence, a deed that can be even more perfect at its next repetition. The story is a ritual, a formal dance, an abstract diagram which expresses more perfectly than any of the other fictions Borges' vision of life as a maze of formal movements whose meaning is unknown. Like the secret Name of God, it may exist, or may be a pure negation.

The incarnation of 'pure reason' on a far more relative level is provided by Don Isidro Parodi, the hero of *Seis problemas para Don Isidro Parodi* (*Six problems of Don Isidro Parodi*, 1943) written in collaboration by Borges and Bioy Casares. Don Isidro, a most original detective figure, is himself serving a gaol sentence for some racecourse crime. The problems have therefore to be brought to him in his cell, and can only be solved by reason, since he cannot visit the scenes of the various crimes. Don Isidro is a well-drawn Buenos Aires type, who knows his way through the suburbs and all the various national minorities that make up the city's population. The language of *Six Problems* is racy and truly *porteno* (of Buenos Aires). The pseudonymous author, H. Bustos Domecq, has an ear for the cadences of local speech far more subtle than Borges' when he is working alone. He has claimed in interview that he and Bioy Casares function perfectly together, composing almost as one man. Yet had one no knowledge of the novels written by Bioy Casares alone, one could guess that Borges provided the strange events, the parade of rare erudition that we find in *Ficciones*, and that Bioy Casares added a sense of character and of language that is sometimes carried to extravagance. The most extreme example of this Argentinianism is the collaborators' story 'El hijo de su amigo' ('His Friend's Son') published in the magazine *Número* of Montevideo in 1952. Here the language is so profoundly unSpanish that it fulfils Borges' most extreme claims in the early essays for the existence of an authentic Argentinian tongue. *Six Problems* belongs less eccentrically to the city, and for an English parallel one need look no further than the American idiom of O. Henry, who had an equal power of coining phrases based on the vernacular pithier than anything to be heard in the bars.

A handful of poems, for the first time in conventional metres, various essays contributed to *Sur*, and a good deal of ephemeral book reviewing complete Borges' work up to the time of the publication of *Ficciones* in 1944. The most important are two poems touching on the theme of recurrence and of Borges' own destiny in South America. These are 'La noche cíclica' ('Cyclical night') of 1940 and 'Poema conyectural' (Conjectural poem) of 1943. These have all the power of the somewhat earlier 'Insomnia'. In them philosophical speculation is raised by nightmare to the height of passion.

> I do not know if we shall return in a second cycle, as
> the figures of a periodic fraction return; But I know
> that an obscure Pythagorean whirling leaves me night
> after night at a point in the world lying somewhere in
> the suburbs. A remote street-corner that may be in the
> the north, the south or the west, but it has always a
> sky-blue plaster wall, a gloomy fig-tree and a broken
> pavement.

These poems revert to Borges' familiar themes. But despite their power they lack fundamental originality. The reminiscences of Baudelaire, Rossetti and perhaps James Thomson are probably involuntary. Whereas all references to past literature in the stories are deliberate, a conscious method of anchoring an anecdote or speculation in a tradition whose monuments line the library walls of this speculative poet.

6   More *Ficciones*

Between the publication of *Ficciones* (1944) and that of his second book of stories *El Aleph* (1949), Borges became concerned with politics and, without premeditation, embarked on a course that was to make him an international figure. In the nineteen years since his second visit to Spain his links with the world outside Argentina had become weak. In Spain, a new literary generation had sprung up that owed something to Ultraism but quickly advanced beyond it. The Civil War had severed all connections. In the anthology *Laurel*, the most influential and best balanced collection of modern poets writing in Spanish, he was represented by poems selected from his three published books. But, in this collection, he was not outstanding. He seemed in comparison with Antonio Machado, García Lorca and César Vallejo—to name but three of the anthology's inclusions—to lack a personal style. But for his references to Buenos Aires, it would have been difficult to distinguish Borges' reflective dream poetry from that of other excellent but limited poets included in *Laurel*. The case of *Ficciones* was entirely different. No one could confuse these stories with those of any other writer, and immediately the French critic Roger Caillois began to publicise and translate them. The time, of course, was inappropriate. It was the year of the Normandy landings and the liberation of Paris. Nevertheless *Ficciones* was available in French almost as soon as in Spanish.

At home Borges published his collected poems in 1943, and these too found a devoted though critical French translator, Néstor Ibarra. While working on the stories of *El Aleph*, Borges continued to collaborate with Bioy Casares, compiling an anthology of detective fiction and some fantasies and crime stories which were not published. From 1945 onwards he was in increasing political difficulty.

Throughout the World War, Borges had been an outspoken

supporter of the Allies. As a leading member and afterwards president of the Argentinian Society of Writers, he was equally outspoken in his opposition to the dictatorial ambitions of the young army officer Juan Perón and his unscrupulous and politically astute wife Eva. Borges saw in Perón a second Rosas, the enemy of the oligarchs in the nineteenth century. Perón had learnt something from the Nazis. He and Eva collected a working-class following, were popular with the small shopkeepers and with the younger officers in the inflated Services. They attacked the oligarchs and big business. The Americans made the mistake of trying to exercise their influence against him in the elections of 1945, and Perón won a striking victory.

In Borges' eyes, Perón was a boor, and the dictatorship exercised by him and his wife was different from the various dictatorships that had prevailed throughout Argentinian history. Borges and his fellow intellectuals of the *Sur* group attempted to oppose Perón with protests and demonstrations. Borges' mother and sister were arrested in one of these, and various intellectuals suffered brief periods of arrest during the Perón epoch. Certainly anti-intellectualism played some slight part in Perón's policies. But many younger men with leftwing sympathies adopted a less intransigent standpoint than that of *Sur*, hoping that the pressure of events would drive Perón towards socialism.

Perón exercised a dictatorship over the Press, suspending one of the two major newspapers, *La Prensa*, and so cutting down the circulation of the second, *La Nación*, by limiting its paper supplies that it became almost unobtainable except by subscribers in 1950. The dictator closed the Society of Writers. With Borges he dealt by way of insult. The Municipality of Buenos Aires was instructed to transfer the poet from his office in the library to the post of Inspector of poultry in the municipal markets. Borges promptly resigned. He was now forced to find an alternative livelihood. He began to lecture on literary subjects in various cities of Argentina and Uruguay, he taught American literature in the Colegio Libre, and was appointed Professor of English literature by the Association for English Culture, a school supported by the British Council. Though his public lectures were sometimes attended by a police invigilator, and he was sometimes followed in the street by a detective, who found his habit of taking long walks annoying, Borges suffered no more than insults and inconvenience from the Peronist regime. When I met him in 1953, in the week following the Peronists' burning down of the Jockey Club, the reputed headquarters of the oligarchs, he was in fear of arrest, and many of his friends, among them Victoria Ocampo, were in jail. He took me on one of his habitual long walks, discoursed on Stevenson and Chesterton, and theories of time and recurrence, and on leaving me at my station, the 'Retiro' (then briefly renamed 'Presidente Perón'), proclaimed aloud in English: 'I never thought that this thing could happen in my country.' In fact, Borges' chief concern in those ten years of dictatorship was the writing of *El Aleph*, just as his chief topic in his conversations with me was the possibility that his stories might be published in London. I brought them back from Argentina, but failed to find a publisher for them.

The stories of *El Aleph* in no way reflect the changed political circumstances in which they were written. Time, identity and the relation of truth and fiction continue to be Borges' chief themes. But in this collection he is far more concerned than in *Ficciones* with the subject of mysticism, already treated in 'The Approach to Al-Mutasim' and 'The Circular Ruins'.

The story which touches most nearly on a contemporary topic is 'Deutsches Requiem', a study in Nazi self-annihilation, which some hasty critics read as a justification of Nazism itself. Otto Dietrich zur Linde is a Prussian aristocrat, a career officer, now on trial as the commander of a concentration camp in which the great Jewish poet David Jerusalem has killed himself. Otto zur Linde has loved Jerusalem's poetry but has let him die. Jerusalem celebrated the world, and praised happiness, which in zur Linde's eyes is a weakness. He has refused to defend himself before the court for War Crimes, and awaits execution. Looking back on Jerusalem's death, zur Linde knows that he had to let him die.

> I do not know whether Jerusalem understood that if I destroyed him, it was to destroy my own compassion. In my eyes he was not a man, not even a Jew; he had been transformed into an area of argument in my own soul.

Zur Linde let Jerusalem die because the poet was a seeker, like the student of Al-Mutasim one open to all experience, while zur Linde was a rigid idealist driven to sacrifice anything that went counter to his ideal of perpetual war. He was even able to accept the destruction of the Third Reich because it would lead, as he believed, to further eras of struggle and war. 'What does it matter,' he concludes, 'if England is the hammer and we the anvil, so long as violence reigns and not servile Christian timidity?' Otto zur Linde seems to echo Milton's fallen angel in his final: 'Let heaven be, even though our place is in hell.'

Borges does not justify zur Linde, though in his person a determined self-reliance may be embodied, whereas in Jerusalem there is a pantheistic weakness, a readiness to believe in happiness and the value of all experience. In addition, however, a third force is adumbrated in the figure of Walt Whitman, admired by both the Prussian and the Jew. 'Whitman celebrates the Universe' zur Linde reflects, 'in an introductory, general and almost indifferent way; Jerusalem dwells on everything with attentive love. He never falls into the error of enumerations and catalogues.' Yet, through zur Linde, Borges seems to be suggesting that besides self-annihilation in war and self-subordination to each experience and delight, there is a third way of transcendence, embodied in Whitman, whose enumerations and catalogues place the world in relationship with something beyond it. 'Deutsches Requiem' is a penetrating study of fanatical idealism. But it is at the same time a philosophical story which leads further than its ostensible theme.

Several pieces in *El Aleph* appear to be pure narratives, without symbolism or philosophical overtones. Zur Linde, Jerusalem and Whitman represent three diametrically opposite positions, and the story fails in its effect if read purely as the drama of remorseless idealism destroying a poet and with him the poetic life. 'Emma Zunz' seems to offer no such complications. The setting is contemporary Buenos Aires, and the heroine—no other Borges story contains a woman character who is not merely a reflection of some man's passion—is a realistically unexaggerated clerk who revenges her father's disgrace by murdering his betrayer. Her father had been cashier at a textile factory, where he was accused by Lowenthal, another of the employees, of embezzlement. He had fled to Brazil where, as Emma learns from a letter, he has died. She resolves to take her revenge—strictly his revenge—on the man who framed him. Lowenthal is now a partner in the business, for which Emma still works. Slowly she passes the day after she receives the news, in her room, in the street, in a social club, chatting to her girl friends and then disgustedly giving herself to a casual foreign sailor in order to substantiate the story she is going to tell, and all the time waiting for the evening when she knows that she can find the man alone in his factory. There she deliberately murders him. Then she telephones the police, stating that the man had lured her there and raped her, and her story is accepted. A commonplace little thriller, with all the suspense of seeing Emma through her interminable day. Yet the last paragraph gives 'Emmz Zunz' a perhaps to be anticipated Pirandellian twist.

> The story was indeed incredible. But it convinced
> everyone because substantially it was true. Emma
> Zunz's tone was genuine, so was her shame, and so was
> her hatred. Only the circumstances were false, and the
> date and one or two proper names.

Lowenthal had not outraged the girl but her father, and not on the day of his death but many years ago, and Emma's hatred of him dated from the day when he wrongfully accused her father of a crime that he himself committed. Thus her story was substantially true though all the details were false. But the virtue of the tale lies less in its double version of truth than in its suspense. Emma's day is an empty anticipation of the evening punctuated by a moment of horror in the sailor's arms.

The story 'La espera' ('The Waiting') is an extended account of the horror of empty time. The anonymous person whom we see taking a room at a boarding house in an ugly street, where Creoles have made way for Italians and Italians for Jews, has fled from some confederates whom he has in some way cheated and who are undoubtedly pursuing him from one hide-out to the next. But in deserting his partners, he has at the same time deserted himself. He is now nobody, a mere expectation of their revenge. He dreams of it every night, and when in the end two men enter his room, he asks them to wait and lies down on the bed to continue his dream.

Did he do this to arouse pity in his killers, or because it is less hard to endure a frightful happening than to imagine it and endlessly await it, or—and this is perhaps more plausible—in order that his assassins should be a dream, as they had so often been, in this same place, at this same hour?

He was performing this act of magic when the shots obliterated him.

The word 'obliterated' confirms him in his nothingness. That a man can be nothing is the burden of another story of Argentinian life, 'El muerto' ('The Dead Man'). The man does not seem to be dead at the opening of the story when he joins a gang of smugglers operating on the Brazilian frontier. He is a nondescript town boy of nineteen, 'a wretched town boy with no other virtue than an infatuation with courage.' Benjamín Otálora wants to be a strong man, a gang leader, yet all the time he is empty, dead. He attaches himself to the smugglers' chief, undertakes the most dangerous jobs, and covets his chief's possessions, his red-haired mistress, his bay horse with its ornate silver trappings. When the boss is away, Otálora takes to giving orders. He usurps the boss's authority, suborns his second in command, rides his horse and sleeps with his woman. But on the last night of the year, when the gang are drinking, the scene is suddenly reversed. As the clock strikes twelve, the boss reasserts his authority, orders the woman obscenely to kiss her new lover and when she tries to resist, flings her on top of him. Then Otálora realises.

> that he has been betrayed from the start and that he has been condemned to death, that they have only allowed him love and command and glory because they already thought of him as dead, because for Bandeira (the boss) he was already a dead man.
>
> Almost contemptuously Suárez (the second man) fired.

Since what point in the story had Otálora been a dead man? Since he had begun to assume authority, or since he had attached himself to these gauchos, men of real 'virtue' who are not infatuated with courage?' Benjamín Otálora is a hollow man, as was the nameless fugitive in the boarding house, as Emma Zunz was not, as the Irish leader was not in 'Theme of the Traitor and the Hero', when he acted the drama of his own assassination in order to provide his country with a spurious hero.

It is the myth that lives on, the reality that dies in 'La otra muerte' ('The Other Death'). A gaucho, Pedro Damián, shows cowardice in his youth and survives a battle in which he might have died as a hero. All his life till his death in old age, he regrets this moment at which he might have transcended his common-place existence. He prays to God to expunge his later years and so change events that he in fact dies that day on the battlefield. God grants him his prayer, but even He cannot alter the past. He has to work, like Herbert Quain, the failed novelist of Borges' earlier story, from the present backwards, from effect to cause. He has to wipe out from the minds of all his neighbours the image of that Damián who survived the battle. Thus He gives the old man his 'other death'.

> It was four in the afternoon. The regular infantry had dug themselves in on the top of the hill; our men charged them with lances. Damián led the charge, shouting, and a bullet struck him full in the chest. He stood in his stirrups, ended his battle cry, and then rolled to the ground, where he lay under the horses' hooves. He died and Masoller's last charge trampled his body. He was so brave, and not yet twenty.

The myth, in ironic technicolour, would be complete, but for the fact that Borges the narrator knows that Damián died of a lung infection as an old man. The story therefore is oblique, and tells not how God worked the miracle and created the myth, but how Borges, by reference to his favourite theologians and meta-physicians, succeeded in seeing how it was done.

'Biografía de Isidro Cruz (1829–1874') is, like 'The End' in *Ficciones* and one or two subsequent stories, a pendant to the epic *Martín Fierro*. At the climax of Hernández's poem, the chief of the mounted police who are pursuing Fierro, the outlaw, changes sides, defends Fierro and saves his life. This story of Borges retells the policeman's change of heart, and shows this to be the moment in which he recognised his destiny. Borges here returns to his obsessive idea that the only moment when a man escapes the cycle of recurrence in which his life or lives pass is that in which he makes this recognition: 'The moment had been waiting for him all his life. In it he understood that his real destiny was to be a lone wolf, not one of a pack of dogs. He understood that the other man (Fierro) was himself.'

The story-teller is at pains to point out that one destiny is no better than another; Cruz did acquire virtue by joining the party to which his father, whom he had never known, had belonged. The sole virtue lay in this moment of truth that had been waiting for him all his life and that was indeed the sum of his life.

Failure to recognise such a fundamental truth is the subject of 'Los teólogos' ('The Theologians'). Aurelian and John of Pannonia are rival theologians or heresiarchs at the Imperial Court. The Huns have destroyed the libraries but a few books survive. From a copy of Plutarch's dialogue on the cessation of the oracles, Aurelian discovers his theory of the Wheel of cyclical time and decides to refute it, in order to anticipate his rival John. John of Pannonia briefly refutes his rival's refutation. Both vindicate the Cross and demolish the Wheel. Nevertheless 'they continued their secret battle. Both served in the same army, coveted the same reward, warred against the same enemy.' But neither wrote a word which was not, secretly, directed against the other. Their whole labours were devoted to their invisible duel. Finally Aurelian triumphs; on his accusation his rival is convicted of heresy and burned at the stake. Aurelian has to witness the execution, but keeps his eyes lowered: 'When he looked up he saw for the first time the face of that hated heretic. It reminded him of someone, but he could not remember of whom'. Aurelian does not regret his rival's death; he feels only relief. Yet for the rest of his life he can only roam the Empire, and dies one rainy night in distant Hibernia. The epilogue takes place in heaven, 'where there is no time'.

> It might be correct to say that Aurelian conversed with God, and that He was so little interested in religious disputes that He took him for John of Pannonia. This

however would imply a confusion in the divine mind.
It would be more correct to say that in Paradise
Aurelian learnt that for the unfathomable Divinity he
and John of Pannonia (the orthodox and the heretic,
the hater and the hated, the accuser and the victim)
formed one single person.

The someone of whom Aurelian was reminded when he saw
John burning was himself. He saw his own face in his victim's and
himself struggled as the other man was tied to the stake. The two
men's destiny was to be one; their lifetime of rivalry was a
delusion, an aberration, in which Aurelian had been the active,
John the passive partner. In 'Historia del guerrero y de la cautiva'
('Story of the Warrior and the Captive'), two incidents distant in
history are narrated which are, in Borges' eyes, the two faces of
the same coin: a German warrior deserts his people for the
civilisation of Rome; an English girl, captured on Argentina's
Indian frontier, refuses a chance to escape from the tribe among
whom she now lives and return to the civilisation of the city.
The latter story is one that Borges had heard from his grandmother, the former a fiction a little reminiscent of Kipling.

Even more patently influenced by Kipling is 'El hombre en el
umbral' ('The Man on the Threshold'), whose leading figure
Glencairn is a tough Scotsman who has been sent to put down the
disorders in an Indian city. He is kidnapped and another officer
is sent to trace him who, now an official of the British Council in
Buenos Aires, is made to tell the story to Borges and Bioy Casares.
The young officer Christopher Dewey finds that throughout the
city there is a conspiracy of silence. Everyone, he feels, is impli-
cated, and no one will speak of Glencairn's disappearance.
Finally he comes to a house where some Muslim ceremony is in
progress. An old man in rags, motionless as a stone, is lying on the
threshold. Dewey asks him if he knows anything of Glencairn, and
the old man begins a story about an English judge long ago, before
the Mutiny, who had wronged the people of a city. These people
had kidnapped him, hidden him in some stables, summoned all
those he had abused to give evidence against him, and after
sentence by a crazy beggar, had executed him with the headsman's
sword. The old man stops talking, and Dewey, looking up, sees a

bloodstained sword being carried across the courtyard. The guests at the ceremony disperse.

Going in he finds Glencairn's body in the stables behind the house. The guests have been the witnesses against Glencairn, and the old man's story of long ago has been told only to prevent Dewey from rescuing Glencairn. But is this realistic explanation sufficient? Is not the old man's tale to be read as one of recurrence? The same thing has happened in the past; and Glencairn and the old man, who is perhaps the beggar who sentenced the earlier judge, maybe also the man who condemned Glencairn, are figures in a repeated pattern. Glencairn stands for the active violent justice of the English, the beggar for the blind yet subtle justice of India. No story of Borges is ever free from ambiguities and parallels, and tricks with time. Borges admits the temporal trickiness of this tale. But the reader must be careful not to read too many hidden significances into it. For it is almost a 'plain tale' in Kipling's sense of the term.

'La busca de Averroes ('Averroes Search') is also a 'plain tale' of a great mind's defeat by an idea that lies outside its experience. The Arab philosopher Averroes wishes to understand the meanings of comedy and tragedy, of which he has read in Aristotle. But the world of the Koran knows nothing of theatres. Puzzled, Averroes attends a feast, where a returning traveller tells of the roses of Hindustan and of a 'house of painted wood' to which he was taken by Moslem merchants, presumably in China.

> 'The persons on the terrace were playing the drum and the lute', (says the traveller) 'save for some fifteen or twenty (with crimson-coloured masks) who were praying, singing and conversing. They were imprisoned, but you could not see the prison, they rode horses, but you could not see the horses; they fought but their swords were canes; they died, and then jumped to their feet again.'

Averroes can no more understand the nature of a theatre than could the traveller himself. He returns home and writes a completely false explanation of comedy and tragedy.

> I felt (writes Borges in the final paragraph) that my
> tale was a symbol of the man I was as I wrote it, and
> that in order to write that tale I should have been that
> man, and that in order to be that man, I should have
> had to write that tale, and so on to infinity.

Borges feels himself to be as absurd when he tries to imagine an
Arab philosopher imprisoned in his world of the Koran, as was
Averroes when he tried to understand the theatre of the Greeks.
Each man lives isolated in the maze of his own conceptions, condi-
tioned by his own civilisation, his own experience, his own reading
But there is a deeper isolation of which Borges speaks in his up-
side-down version of a Greek tale.

'La casa de Asterión' ('The House of Asterion') is a retreat-
ment of the story of Theseus, who penetrated the Cretan labyrinth
to kill the Minotaur. But it is told from the Minotaur's viewpoint.
He is the bull Asterion, who looks forward to death as a redemp-
tion. The house is the labyrinth, in which he is isolated although
all its doors are open. In fact, the labyrinth is the loneliness of a
man's mind. All things are reflected in it, and though there seem
to be no confining doors, there is no escape, only the distant hope of
a redeemer. Every nine years, nine men visit Asterion that 'he may
deliver them from all evil'. He hears their steps joyfully, he rushes
to meet them. But 'the ceremony is short.' He kills them. One
thinks of the Ancient Mariner condemned to kill the thing he
loves. He wonders whether his redeemer will be a creature like
himself. He is not. He is merely the commonplace Theseus, who
says at the story's conclusion: 'Would you believe it, Ariadne?
The Minotaur hardly defended himself.' Such, Borges seems to
say, is the sadness of mental isolation, in a maze everything seems
to repeat itself endlessly, and those who come to visit the poet, the
creator of the sun itself, are killed by his coldness.

Two interlocking stories which are also concerned with labyrinths, 'Abenjacán el Bojarí, muerto en su laberinto' ('Ibn-
Hakam al-Bokhari, Dead in his Labyrinth') and 'Los does reyes y
los dos laberintos ('The Two Kings and the Two Labyrinths'), do
not justify detailed analysis. A crime takes place in the Arabian
desert. A treasure is stolen, one thief is killed or abandoned by the
other. One of the thieves (but which?) builds a labyrinthine house

on the English coast, either as a hiding place or a conspicuous lure to attract his fellow thief—who in this case survives his abandonment in the desert. The local parson preaches a Sufi sermon about labyrinths, and how to escape from them This is the content of the second story. It is as if Borges were parodying himself. A hint from 'The Garden of Forking Paths', a touch of the Arabian Nights, and some memories of Wilkie Collins' *The Moonstone* combine to form the single failure in the *El Aleph* volume, the only tale in which Borges tells nothing of himself, but produces only a confusion of crazy hypotheses.

'El Immortal' ('The Immortal') is the finest and most profound of the philosophical stories in *El Aleph*. In the last volume of an eighteenth-century edition of Pope's *Iliad* is found an account, presumably translated from the Latin, of a Roman expedition from Egypt across the desert in search of the legendary City of the Immortals. The expedition falls away; some die of fever or thirst, and some mutiny and turn back. Finally Marcus Flaminius Rufus, Roman tribune and writer of the memoir, is left alone. He lies down alone within sight of the 'pyramids and towers' of the City and dreams.

> My dream was unbearable; I dreamt of a tiny, glistening labyrinth, in the centre of which was a water jar. My hands almost touched it, my eyes saw it. But the curves of the labyrinth were so intricate and confused, that I should die before I could reach it.

There is a double symbolism here; the labyrinth is the City, which is in fact an underground maze, and the 'pure' water in the jar stands for the immortality that the Roman tribune is seeking. The dream, however, is a nightmare. When he wakes, he drinks of the 'impure' waters of Immortality and sees the Immortals and their City. The City is the vast underground ruin of a labyrinth, built long ago and now deserted, and the Immortals are brutish sub-men, troglodytes who have lost the gift of speech. The City of the Immortals is like the Library of Babel, a nightmare hell. Marcus Flaminius is alone. His habitual world has slipped from him with his deserting soldiers. He is alone, and therefore, as if dead. All human experiences have vanished. There are not even words to express this state of Immortality, which is utter negation of the 'real' world. Immortality is a curse, and the men who discovered it built a hideous stone prison, which they then deserted to sink into brutishness.

One troglodyte attaches himself to Marcus Flaminius. This 'Immortal' has all knowledge and therefore cannot turn his mind to any isolated thought. He is 'memorious', though not after the manner of Funes, since ordinary facts seem to have escaped him. The creature's humility and wretchedness and his devotion to the Roman stranger remind Marcus Flaminius of Argos, Ulysses' old dog in the *Odyssey*. He calls him Argos. He tries to teach him to speak. At last the poor creature weeps and stammers a few words of Greek: 'Argos, Ulysses' dog'. The two Immortals, the Roman and the troglodyte, direct their steps backwards towards mortality. Homer – for Marcus Flaminius believes the troglodyte once to have been Homer, since he remembers fragmentarily the poems—tells him the story of the City's building, nine hundred years before, of its destruction by its builders and of their retreat into the caves. Gradually Homer's memory returns, and the two men set out in search of the 'pure' water, which is that of mortality. Homer disappears, in some way coalescing into the Roman, but Marcus Flaminius finds the water and returns to the wheel of incarnations. He is at the battle of Stamford Bridge in 1066; he transcribes the Arabian Nights and plays chess in Samarkand; he practises astrology in India and again in Bohemia. In Aberdeen he subscribes to the six volumes of Pope's Homer, mentioned at the beginning of the story. In 1921 he becomes the bookseller who sold these volumes to Borges' friend. Leaving his ship on the African coast, on his way to Bombay, the bookseller finds a spring of clear water and scratches his hand on a thorn. He now knows that he is truly mortal and, remembering all his past experiences, writes down this account of his journey to the City. Seemingly, when he died at sea, he found release from the wheel: 'I have been Homer; shortly I shall be No One, like Ulysses; in short I shall be all men, I shall be dead.' Borges concludes with one of his mock-scholarly postscripts in which he quotes commentators on the story, real and imaginary. His last word, however, hints at a personal interpretation of immortality:

'When the end draws near,' wrote Cartaphilus (the bookseller), 'there no longer remain any remembered images; only words remain.' Words, disordered and mutilated words, other men's words: these are the poor alms left him by the hours and the centuries.

The end is an ironic negation. Our only immortality is to be found in the ill-informed comments of our successors. Mortality is best, and when we we are released from that we sink into oblivion or nothingness. We become, at best, the subject of disorderly speculation. As artists we are entombed in the comments of our critics.

'The Immortal' succeeds, however, as a narrative; even the reflective middle section with its definitions of immortality holds the reader. One might read it as one reads Rider Haggard's *She*, enjoying it as a tale of African adventure, of a search for a magic city across the desert, and of the many incarnations of a Time traveller in the Wellsian sense. It is a splendid adventure story. But it is also an ironic refutation of religious hope, in a writer whose every story is secretly concerned, as 'The Immortal' is openly, with the subject of immortality or transcendence.

7 The 'Mystical' Experience

In all the many interviews that Borges has given to critics and admirers he has never referred to his religious beliefs, has never indeed suggested that he has any. My own attempts to open the subject in 1953 were brusquely repulsed. It is true that he talked about the mystics, but as writers who recorded certain curious experiences, whose statements concerning time and timelessness, recurrence, cosmology had a great speculative interest for him, but nothing more. He did not admit to any personal concern with such things.

Yet so many of Borges' stories, in particular the three that will be the subject of this chapter—'The Aleph' itself, 'The Zahir' and 'La escritura del dios' ('The God's Script')—firmly contradict Borges' defensive denial of personal involvement in this matter. In 'The Approach to Al-Mutasim' the student spends his life in search of a master, whom he finally finds behind the curtain. In the stories that immediately follow Borges' illness, various labyrinthine hells are elaborated from which there is no escape. Somewhere there is a clue, but it cannot be found and interpreted. Again, in many of the stories, a man's life has a meaning that is not known to him. He is different from others, and he merges into others. He may write another man's book or wage a lifelong battle with another only to learn in the end that the two are one. In all the stories, there is at least a hint of nightmare, or rather of insomnia punctuated by fragmentary catnaps of nightmare. Once Borges confessed to an interviewer that the writing of 'Funes the Memorious' had rid him of insomnia, that is to say that in creating this memory-haunted peasant he had in some way disposed of haunting memories that disturbed his sleep. Analysing his stories and essays, one finds that his chief preoccupation is always with heresies of a Gnostic kind. His references to Christianity or Buddhism, to Plato, Swedenborg, the Sufis, show a fascination with magic, and particularly with the magical moment, which is identified in his poetry with the moment of *déjà vu* in which he first saw the pink painted street corner in the Buenos Aires suburb, and to other such moments in childhood or in his nocturnal walking in which things looked different; moments, one may say, in which 'time stopped', as it did for Hladik when he faced the firing squad in 'The Secret Miracle'. We may leave the subject of Borges' personal involvement in this area with the remark that he shows an uncanny familiarity with the stages of the mystic search for one only speculatively interested in such matters.

The clue may lie in a common object, a copper coin, as it does in 'The Zahir':

> In Buenos Aires, the Zahir is a common twenty centavo piece, on which the letter N and the number 2 are scratched, as if with a razor blade or a penknife. 1929 is the date on the obverse side.

So the story opens, and Borges goes on to list the different forms in which the Zahir has appeared in the past in different countries: a tiger, a blind beggar, a compass—motifs that appear in various of his other stories. Later Borges explains why the magic quality should be inherent in a chance coin.

> Money is abstract; money is future time. . . . It is unforeseeable time, Bergsonian time, not the rigid time of Islam or the Stoics. The determinists deny that there is such a thing as a possible act, that is an act that *may* take place; a coin symbolises our free will.

The narrator is handed this coin in his change at a bar in the early hours of one morning, as he is returning from a visit of condolence to the relatives of a woman with whom he has been in love. They have shown him photographs of this girl at different ages, which have left him with a feeling of impermanence and loss of reality. The property of this twenty centavo piece which contains the Zahir (in Arabic, the visible) is that once possessed of it, one cannot get rid of it. One may part with the actual coin, but it still controls one. A young woman is mentioned who, by dint of repeatedly dreaming of such a coin, goes out of her mind. It possesses the narrator, and extends his vision to other dimensions. 'There was a time,' he writes, 'when I could visualise first the obverse, then the reverse. Now I can see both sides at once. Its effect is compulsive, nightmarish. I was unable to change my fixed idea.' The narrator is afraid that the Zahir will drive him mad as it had the poor girl. He calls it up at night certain that he can get rid of it when he wishes. But it stays with him. It obsesses him, but does not make him unhappy. Indeed, he associates with it that power of transcendent vision spoken of by Tennyson. 'If we could understand a single flower' said the English poet, 'we should know who we are and what the world is.' Borges speculates that perhaps Tennyson meant that the visible world is fully present in every phenomenon. In fact, Tennyson was no philosopher, and was referring to a practice of his own, described by his son Hallam in his study of the poet, whereby he induces in himself a slightly altered state of consciousness. The practice of repeating his own name when on solitary walks, no doubt learnt from Fitzgerald who would have met the idea in Sufi writings, gave Tennyson moments of transcendental experience which in 'The Zahir' Borges identifies with a terrifying nightmare: 'One night,' he concludes at the end of his story, 'I shall no longer perceive the Universe, I shall perceive only the Zahir.' Others will think him mad. But by endlessly repeating in Tennyson's manner his own name or the 'ninety-nine divine names', he will perhaps one day wear away the Zahir and: 'perhaps behind the coin I shall find God.'

'The Zahir' is a story of mystical obsession. In several of Borges' stories there occurs the motif of life as a dream, even as a nightmare, and nowhere is this thought more persistently dominant than in 'The Zahir'. But nowhere—not even in 'The Library of Babel' or the description of the abandoned city in 'The Immortal' —is the dream more nightmarish and terrible than in 'The Zahir'. In an essay in *Otras inquisiciones*, Borges writes of Pascal's terror when facing his vision of the universe as a sphere whose centre is everywhere and whose circumference is nowhere. That terror is embodied in this story of a man who, once seized, apparently by chance, by the idea of transcendence, cannot go back to the moment before the coin was passed to him. Perhaps the writer himself was passed this coin in youth, or in those sleepless nights during his illness. But here it is strongly associated with a fear that differs from the awe recorded by Pascal. To lose the dream of life, no longer to believe in it, is to expose oneself to annihilation, to the dread plunge into the pit of nothingness.

'The Aleph', the title story of Borges' second collection and another of his most masterly pieces, presents an alternative means of cosmic perception to the transcendent vision of 'The Zahir'. In confronting the Aleph, which is not an object, it is possible to receive simultaneous knowledge of all things at once, not as disparate memories, as in Funes' case, but in unity. The idea for the Aleph itself came, I believe, from a passage in the biography of Jakob Boehme which describes his first illumination of 1599. It is quoted by William James in his *Varieties of Religious Experience*.

> Sitting one day in his room, his eyes fell on a burnished pewter dish, which reflected the sunlight with such marvellous splendour that he fell into an inward ecstasy, and it seemed to him that he could now look into the principles and deepest foundations of things. He believed that it was only a fancy, and in order to banish it from his mind he went out upon the green. But here he remarked that he gazed into the very heart of things, the very herbs and grass, and that actual nature harmonised with what he had inwardly seen.

The Aleph itself is not a solid object like Boehme's pewter dish, which aroused in him a spiritual vision that never afterwards left him. It is a radiance perceived in a cellar, beneath a staircase:

> 'On the underpart of the stairs, towards the right, I saw a small irridescent sphere of almost unbearable brightness. At first I thought it spun round; then I realised that this was an illusion produced by the dizzying visions contained in it. The Aleph's diameter might be two or three centimetres, but all cosmic space was within it, actual and undiminished. Everything (a

mirror glass for example) was an infinity of things, for
I clearly saw everything from every angle of the
Universe. I saw the teeming sea, I saw dawn and
night, I saw the hordes of America, I saw a silver
cobweb in the centre of a black pyramid, I saw a
broken labyrinth (in London), I saw endless eyes near-
to, watching themselves in me as in a mirror, I saw all
the mirrors on earth and none of them reflected me . . .'

The visionary saw everything, and was himself not there. He is
the same Borges who took the small coin in his change. But this
time it is another woman that he mourns, and her name—
Beatriz—is meant to remind us of Dante's lost love in whom, in
La vita nuova, he incarnated his intellectual vision of the universe.
'The Aleph' is a more complex story than 'The Zahir' since it
contains a secondary character, Carlos Argentino Daneri, who is
psychologically related to the narrator Borges. He is first cousin of
the lost Beatriz, he is a librarian and poet, and it is he who first
discovers the vision in the cellar, to which he introduces the
narrator. He is the author of a vast cataloguing poem in cantos,
the inspiration for which he has derived from a careful memorising
of all that he has seen in this magic mirror. The poem is immensely
dull, but a published selection from it comes second in the
National prize for literature, whereas Borges' book of poems
The Sharper's Cards does not gain a single vote. There is a memory
here of Borges' second place in the Municipal competition of
1929.

The Aleph, which Borges suggests at the close of the story was
probably a false Aleph, appears to give in its seemingly revolving
but actually still mirror a vision of things and events, not actually
temporal, but received by the gazer as successive. It nourishes his
memory, but is in danger of over-filling his mind, of making him
memorious, like Funes. When the narrator no longer sees the
Aleph his memories of Beatriz fade. In itself it is obsessive like
the Zahir. How to get rid of the Aleph? There is no problem,
as there was for the Zahir. A firm of demolishers are waiting to
pull down the house, and the Aleph is inherent in a single stone
in the cellar. The intellectual mirror will be lost in a builder's
yard.

Like 'The Zahir' the story of 'The Aleph' is nightmare. Though the idea for the visionary sphere may have been suggested by Boehme's illumination, the working of the Aleph is very different, reminding us as it does of some magic object in the *Arabian Nights*. Borges appears not to have reflected on the unitive vision of the saints, which is a looking into the roots of things. 'In that single gigantic instant,' he writes, 'I saw millions of cats, both delightful and terrible; and not one of them surprised me as much as the fact that they all occupied the same point, without overlapping or transparency.' Boehme, who had experienced this unitive vision, would not thus have sought for a metaphor.

'The Zahir' and 'The Aleph' describe false ways of inducing vision which, as Borges admits, produce false or partial, and always terrible, experiences. In one story alone in his two volumes, '*La escritura del dios*' ('The God's Script'), does he produce a true statement about the mystical path. The priest of an Aztec cult lies in prison, yearning to take revenge for his people upon their Spanish conquerors. In the next cell, divided from him by bars, is a striped tiger—the American jaguar. The prison is dark except at brief moments of the day, when his food is lowered to him through a hatch. He knows that all power will be his if he can discover a magic formula, written in the handwriting of the god. He calls up memories. Gradually he transforms his mind into a kind of Aleph.

> I imagined the first morning of time. I imagined my god
> confiding the message to the bright skins of jaguars,
> who would endlessly couple and engender in caves and
> reed-beds and on islands, so that the last man should
> receive it. I imagined this chain of jaguars, this
> labyrinth of jaguars, terrorising meadows and flocks in
> order to preserve a design.

In the brief intervals of light, the priest studies the jaguar's skin. For long years, he observes and visualises the creature's markings. But he discovers that no god could write a sentence there. He dreams a dream within a dream, like that of that other priest in 'The Circular Ruins'. The dream becomes a nightmare, and he returns with relief to the reality of his damp prison.

83

> . . . I blessed the darkness and the stone.
> Then came something that I can neither forget nor
> describe. There came union with the divinity, with the
> Universe. . . . I saw a very tall wheel, that not before
> my eyes or behind them, or on either side, but
> everywhere at once. . . . It was made of things future,
> present and past, woven together, and I was one of the
> threads in this total web.

The priest has received his vision. He possesses the word of
power but has no wish to use it, for he knows that he and his
Spanish tormentors are one. Finally he speaks of himself as
another.

> That man *has been he*, but now he does not care. Why
> should he care for the fate of that other, why should he
> care for that other man's people, if he is now nobody?
> For this reason I do not pronounce the formula. For
> this reason I let the days forget me, stretched out in the
> dark.

The note of acceptance had already been struck in 'The Circular Ruins', the acceptance of a cosmic order, in which past,
present and future are one and in which a myth or a rite is a rediscovery and an acquiescence in a pre-existing world pattern.
Like 'The Circular Ruins', this story is free of circumstantial
detail, and of references to books and persons and philosophical
theories. But it depends as much as the other stories on literary
inspiration. The dark prison is the Cave of Plato's myth, and the
priest's change of heart is that of Coleridge's Mariner when 'the
trance is abated.' It is not the divine acceptance of the *Bhagavadgita*, the resolve henceforth to act without thought for results,
whether gain or loss. The Aztec priest resigns himself, accepting
non-being and non-action; his people remain unavenged on their
conquerors to this day.

Borges published this second collection in 1949, and added one
or two of the lesser pieces to an augmented edition in 1957.
But his main period of fiction writing was over. The scar of his
illness of Christmas 1938 had healed over, and the writing of these

several versions of existential nightmare had no doubt assisted in his cure. Borges accepted his stories, and on the whole rejected his poetry. In 1953 he was unwilling to speak of himself as a poet. Indeed, in a poem of that time, '*Mateo XXV:30*', which stands with 'Poema conyectural' among his best, he speaks of himself as 'the unprofitable servant'.

> Days with more people than Balzac, the scent of
> honeysuckle,
> Love and its anticipatory vigil and unbearable
> memories,
> Sleep like a buried treasure, bountiful chance
> And memory itself, that man cannot look on clear-
> headed,
> All this was given you, and also
> The food of the heroes of old:
> Betrayal, defeat, humiliation.
> In vain we have squandered the ocean on you,
> In vain the sun, seen through the marvelling eyes of
> Whitman;
> You have wasted the years and they have wasted you,
> And still you have not written the poem.

It is a sad epitaph on Borges' greatest creative period. Yet the poem expresses a frustration that can be seen throughout the two volumes of stories. Essentially they are dry, lacking in human feeling, even in intellectual fire. For always, like Pascal, he feels the terror of visionary discovery and, unlike Pascal, seeks immediate shelter behind the Chinese wall of his books. Each idea can be countered by a contrary idea. The labyrinth may, like the minotaur's, be open on all sides. Yet it is necessary to dream up walls, to remain in the comparative safety of the dark, harried only by nightmares. For Borges, every religion is invalidated by its heresies. He cannot believe, and in his books finds generous sustenance for his unbelief.

8   Shrouded Mirrors

The first half of the Fifties saw the founding of Borges' international reputation with the publication of *Labyrinths,* a selection of his stories, in Paris. At home, he continued his battle with the Perón regime, which drove him from his fastness in the Society of Writers, and finally closed that organisation. But the Perón regime had far greater difficulties to contend with than were presented by a handful of conservative writers: inflation, a flourishing black market, and urgent demands from the urban working class from which Perón drew his chief support. He had given the workers higher wages and legal protection against dismissal. Countrymen flocked to the towns in search of factory jobs, and squatted in shanties on waste lots. Production of meat fell, and on meat exports Argentina depended for its living. Perón looked for help in developing Argentina's oil resources. Only the United States could provide it, and Perón's popularity depended on his anti-Americanism. Moreover his wife Eva was dead and she, with her much vaunted programmes of social security—financed by forced gifts from the business corporations—had always been a more popular figure than the President. The officers of the armed forces retained their power, and supported Perón only so long as he could offer them advantages. He ceased to do so, and in 1955 was swept aside by an armed coup. Borges spoke of it as a glorious revolution. It was a mere return to the pre-Peronist era.

The new government appointed Jorge Luis Borges head of the National Library in response to a proposal from the management of *Sur* and a petition by the newly reopened Society of Writers. The appointment was so suitable that no other candidate was named, and the Peronist incumbent did not even return to the Library to collect his papers. In the next year, Borges was appointed Professor of English and American literature at the

University of Buenos Aires. Here he taught a general literary course, 'from *Beowulf* to Bernard Shaw', for twelve years. His interest in the Anglo-Saxon poems had begun long ago. Through his Haslam grandmother he felt a personal affinity with them, and though he has never mastered the language—indeed he reads it with a modern German accent—he has made of it and of the sagas a close poetic study. The Icelandic sagas, the Saxon bards, and the nineteenth century Argentinian poets who celebrated the gauchos all arouse his enthusiasm. They are for him the primitives, poets of violent action, in contrast to the moderns, of whom he knows himself to be so exaggerated an example, for whom all experience is inward and intellectual.

In the course of the Fifties, Borges published a brief introduction to the gaucho poetry (1951) which is included in recent editions of *Discusión*, a two-volume collection of the poems themselves, compiled in collaboration with Bioy Casares, and a primer of ancient Germanic literatures, also a work of collaboration, published in Mexico. Collaboration had now become Borges' habitual practice, for after the last of a series of eight eye operations, his powers of reading almost totally failed. The essay on Germanic literatures, contributed to a scholarly Mexican series, can have drawn little but its general ideas from this Argentinian amateur of ancient letters. On the other hand, the long and extremely destructive essay on Leopoldo Lugones (1955) is so patently his own that in the reprint of 1965 he takes full credit for it, merely acknowledging his collaborator—who can have been no more than an amanuensis—on the fly-leaf. Most of his collaborations were with Bioy Casares, and these included two film scripts, published but never screened. For the rest of her long life his mother acted as his reader and secretary and, through her efforts, he continued to 'read' all the books he needed. The 1955 'revolution' gave Borges his true place as the leading writer of Argentina. A doctorate of letters and the National Prize for Literature were welcome honours, and year by year the publication continued of his Collected Works, begun in 1952. The collection is deliberately incomplete. Borges says that his chief reason for authorising it was to drop unworthy works from the canon. The three early volumes of essays disappeared almost completely. So did many of the poems from the first three books, though some of his rejects have been restored to favour in the bilingual *Selected Poems 1923–1967*. Because of his blindness, his creative career seemed to be at an end. In 1960, however, when the collected edition was completed, there appeared two new volumes. The first, *Otras Inquisiciones*, was made up of essays contributed to *Sur* and brief sketches of English writers, no doubt the by-products of Borges' teaching. The other new volume entitled *El hacedor* ('The Maker'), however, contains new pieces in verse and prose composed since 1955.

Otras Inquisiciones contains little that is unexpected. Borges returns to his philosophical preoccupation with time, which he endeavours to 'refute' in the manner of his earlier essays on eternity. In dealing with English writers, he is content to speculate on a single aspect which catches his fancy. What exactly did Keats understand by 'eternity' in the Nightingale ode? To what extent was Fitzgerald's *Rubaiyat* an ancient poem? He dwells on Coleridge's interrupted dream of Kubla Khan (now an exploded legend), on Wilde and on Beckford, and in discussion of allegory in the novel shows himself to be completely out of sympathy with the novel as an art form.

El hacedor—the title of the English translation is *Dreamtigers*—is, on the other hand, a 'concentration of Borges', made necessary by his changed methods of composition. Hitherto his stories had filled perhaps a dozen pages and despite their brevity contained a great number of digressions and asides, references to books and persons—real and imaginary—and to strange philosophies. The poems of the first three volumes and such later pieces as 'Conjectural Poem' and '*Matthew XXV: 30*' were written in a not very loose 'free verse'. Now, however, that Borges could no longer write, rewrite and alter his work, which has always been very laboriously constructed, he had to write in forms that he could easily remember, turning them over in his head on his walks or in the library and dictating them only when perfect. *Dreamtigers*, therefore, is made up of fables that are two pages long and of poems in regular rhymed forms, many of them sonnets. This new concentration was not unwelcome to Borges, whose poetic taste was becoming more and more classical, and as for his fables or parables, they now became the natural form for speculations no longer agonised. Yet the reflection of past agonies persists. In

'Los espejos velados' ('Shrouded Mirrors') Borges tells of his childish fear of mirrors and their reflections. They seemed to 'threaten a spectral duplication or multiplication of reality'. As a young man he told a girl of this childish horror, now outgrown, and many years later heard that this girl had gone mad. He had transferred to her his childish fears and he believed that he was persecuting her. But 'I no longer care,' he concludes. The brief anecdote suggests two themes: the power of the artist to project his myth on another, while himself becoming immune from it by this act of projection; and that the artist is not touched by reality, but constructs substitutes for it. 'Una rosa amarilla' (A Yellow Rose') tells of the poet Marino's illumination on his death-bed.

> Marino saw the rose as Adam might have seen it in Paradise, and realised that it stood in its own eternity, not in his word, and that we can mention or allude to something, but not express it; and that the tall, proud volumes that cast a golden shadow in a corner of his room were not (as his vanity dreamed) a mirror of the world, but one thing more added to the world.

Similarly in 'Parábola del palacio' ('Parable of the Palace') the poet takes the whole of a labyrinthine Eastern palace and concentrates it into a poem of a single line, indeed of a single word, and is executed by the king for his theft. In '*Inferno, I, 32*', the leopard learns that it exists only for this single line of Dante's poem, and Dante, in a dream granted to him as to Marino on his deathbed, learns that he too exists only for the poem.

The poet of failing vision is increasingly aware that objects are fading from him, and sinks deeper into a mythical world made up of platonic ideas created by the poet as myth-maker. But these myths are not eternal; they too will fade. In '*Paradiso, XXXI, 108*', Borges asks whether perhaps the face of Christ may not have faded and God be now not one Man but all of us. Perhaps the disintegration goes further: 'perhaps we may see that face tonight in the labyrinths of dream, and will not know in the morning that we saw it.' In 'Ragnarök', Borges and his friends call up the old brutish Germanic gods, and declining to be won over by fear or pity for them shoot them down with revolvers. Here, I think, we may read a political reference. ' "In dreams", writes Coleridge'—so this fable opens—"images represent the sensations we think they cause." ' The decayed old gods incarnate our own ancient terrors. If we allow it, they will return in the form of Hitler, or Perón. So we must extirpate mercilessly what in ourselves calls these images to life.

All the fables in *Dreamtigers* are concerned with the poet as mythmaker, and with the independent power of the myths he creates. He is not merely a creator but exists like Dante solely for the myth he creates. He has no other existence. He is like Shakespeare in 'Everything and Nothing'—the title is in English—who, when he endeavours to escape and become an ordinary person, the small-town usurer of Stratford, is forced to take on the role of poet afresh each time he receives a visitor from London.

> The story goes that before or after he died, he found himself in God's presence and said: 'I who have been so many men to no purpose, want to be one man, myself.' The voice of God replied from a whirlwind: 'Neither am I one self. I dreamed the world as you dreamed your work, my Shakespeare, and the shapes of my dream are you who, like me, are many persons, and no one.'

The same thing is said in the much quoted parable 'Borges y yo' ('Borges and I'). The whole life of Borges the individual goes to nourish Borges the poet 'who has managed to write some worthwhile pages'. But this Borges, 'news of whom reaches me through the post, and whose name I read on an academic roster, or in a biographical dictionary' is himself impermanent. He cannot justify himself by those pages 'because the good part no longer belongs to anyone, not even to the other one, but to the Spanish language and to tradition' and eventually 'everything belongs to oblivion or to the other one'.

The prose pieces in *Dreamtigers* are resigned. Borges the man consents to sacrifice himself to Borges the poet, even though this personage is himself fictitious and 'cannot save him'. But the mirrors in which Borges saw such terrifying visions of duplicity and multiplicity are now shrouded. They cannot drive him mad as they once did that poor girl, who was perhaps his opposite and double, the girl whom he never loved and about whose fate he does not even care.

The poems in *Dreamtigers* are similarly muted. They are sadder and more personal than the prose pieces, and not one of them has the sweep of Borges' last and greatest poem in his old vein of agonised speculation, 'Poema del cuarto elemento' ('Poem of the fourth element')—water. Here he pursues God in all His changing forms, finds Him finally in the fourth element, and prays that He will not forget Borges:

> De Quincey, in the tumult of dreams, saw
> your ocean of faces and nations turn to stone;
> you have calmed the anguish of the generations,
> you have washed the flesh of my father and of Christ.

> Water, I beseech you. By this dreamy
> web of rhythmic words that I speak,
> Remember Borges, your swimmer, your friend,
> and do not fail his lips at the final moment.

Here the agonised pulse of the poem recalls Unamuno, clamouring before a God in whom he can never finally believe. But the Borges of the later poems no longer clamours. In the poem 'Limites' ('Limits'), Borges regrets that every moment may be his last, that every action he takes may be performed for the last time.

> There is a door you have closed forever
> And some mirror is expecting you in vain;
> To you the crossroads seem wide open,
> But watching you, four-faced, is a Janus.

> *translation by* Alastair Reid

This poem, a little antecedent to those in *El hacedor*, retains a freshness of imagery which is often lacking in the poems that follow. Reversing his original ultraist theory, Borges, as has already been said, had come to believe that the best subjects for poetry were the ancient commonplaces, the *topoi*: death as a sleep, time as a river, life as a dream. These classical metaphors appear in the poem 'Arte poética' in which Borges rehearses his future poetic themes. New attention had been given to these *topoi* by the German critic, Ernst Robert Curtius, whose work Borges probably knew, though he nowhere refers to it. The purpose of a poem, according to Borges' new theory, was to treat an old theme in a slightly new way, to clothe the old metaphors in new words. Thus he turned away from the main line of modern poetry, renouncing everything that stemmed from the French symbolists and reverting to techniques of the eighteenth and nineteenth centuries. In some of his sonnets he echoes Quevedo, though avoiding extreme baroque conceits; one of the best is a fine sonnet on the death in battle of his grandfather Colonel Francisco Borges. The sonnet succeeds, yet smacks of the pastiche; only the Colonel's poncho and his enemies' rifles lift him out of the seventeenth century. Perhaps Borges is more deeply moved when celebrating Elvira de Alvear, a dead lady whom he had loved; but here too seventeenth century echoes are persistent.

> Of Elvira what I saw first years and years
> Past, was her smile and it is now the last.
>
> *translation by* Norman Thomas di Giovanni

One is distressingly reminded of a seventeenth-century complimentary poem, in which the poet sees the dead woman not as herself but as a formal victim of death.

The seventeenth century and the nineteenth alternate in Borges' poems of the Sixties. Contrary to all poetic fashions of the day, he wrote several narrative pieces in rhymed quatrains, which while telling a story at the same time pointed a moral, usually on the subject of poetic creation. In 'El Golem' the rabbi of Prague learns God's secret name, but somehow gets it wrong, so that the man he fashions turns out to be a moron without the gift of speech. In 'Ariosto y los árabes' '(Ariosto and the Arabs') Borges uses an incident from the *Orlando furioso* as a motive for writing an elegy on the poetic imagination, now reduced to a shadow, yet to a shadow more real than the poet himself. Reading Ariosto is for him a more real experience than life itself.

The poems of *El hacedor*, and others of the period, are accomplished and uniformly elegiac. Throughout the Sixties he continued to write poems of this kind that become increasingly 'occasional' as the years pass, referring to his reading, to his past memories, to ancestral happenings and to patriotic themes. Gradually acceptance begins to prevail over lamentation, and God becomes a less enigmatic shadow. Indeed his friend and French translator, Néstor Ibarra, reproaches him for now abandoning his atheism. But was he ever an atheist?

Nowhere is the theme of stoical acceptance better expressed than in the 'Poema de los dones' ('Poem of the gifts') in which he mourns and accepts his blindness. The poem invites comparison with Milton's sonnet on the same theme of affliction, and is not altogether eclipsed by it. Groussac, to whom he refers in his conclusion, was an Argentinian scholar and Borges' predecessor at the beginning of the century as head of the National Library. He too became blind.

> Wandering through the gradual galleries,
> I often feel with vague and holy dread
> I am that other dead one who attempted
> The same uncertain steps on similar days.
>
> Which of the two is setting down this poem—
> A single sightless self, a plural I?
> What can it matter, then, the name that names me,
> Given our curse is common and the same?
>
> Groussac or Borges, now I look upon
> This dear world losing shape, fading away
> Into a pale uncertain ashy-gray
> That feels like sleep, or else oblivion.

translation by Alastair Reid.

Certainly there is no Miltonic affirmation here. Indeed blindness is accepted, if acceptance is the word, as a kind of death, a death which draws together all those whom it afflicts. The concluding note of unreality, of the poet stumbling in the dark

93

galleries of the library, opens out beyond the immediate theme of blindness to a Borgesian vista of man, the creator, seeking a reality that is neither in him nor in the poem created. Another poem in this collection, 'Ahédrez' ('Chess') speaks of God standing behind the player, and asks what ultimate God stands behind God. These poems are at their best when the poet asks those questions that recall the anguish of his stories. But generally the deliberately conventional rhythms and language and the deliberate echoes of the seventeenth and nineteenth centuries muffle their impact. In Néstor Ibarra's opinion, Borges' poems of the Sixties are his best, and the poet would himself agree. But a reader attuned to modern poetry, from Baudelaire to Sylvia Plath and Robert Lowell, will find Borges more convincing and more powerful in his poems of Buenos Aires and those few urgent metaphysical questionings of the Fifties.

The Sixties saw the blossoming of that 'other Borges' the travelling ambassador of Argentinian letters. In 1961, he made his first journey abroad for thirty-six years, visiting the University of Texas on a grant from an American foundation to lecture in Argentinian literature. Here he found himself accepted as a great man, and the University Press immediately undertook the translation and publication of his complete works. Of these, he had some months earlier made a restricted anthology, discarding freely and reducing his eight small volumes of collected works to a single book on which he was prepared to base his reputation. Earlier in the year Borges was awarded also, jointly with Samuel Beckett, the Formentor prize, an international publishers' award given for the first time in that year. At about the same time he was honoured by the Italian government with the title of Commendatore. On his return from Texas, similar honours were conferred on him in Buenos Aires by the Argentine Academy and at the French Embassy. The immediate result was that the stories appeared in English and other translations. In 1963 he and his mother made a grand tour of Europe, receiving special honours in Madrid. A military coup which unseated the nominally democratic President in Buenos Aires left him unmoved.

During his first visit to England, Borges gave a couple of lectures on the gaucho poets and, under British Council guidance, made a number of pilgrimages to the homes of admired dead authors, to Henry James' house at Rye, to the homes of Kipling and H. G. Wells. Though he was now too blind to appreciate details, he claimed to be sensitive to atmosphere. One felt that, compensating for his blindness and in accordance with a tendency to reduce everything to the level of thought that had been his from youth, Borges lived a completely internal life. He freely answered his interviewers with confidences which were not confidences, and courteously fenced with anyone who tried to penetrate his guard. My own interview with him for the Third Programme elicited well-rehearsed answers, and a self-deprecatory refusal to admit that his stories betrayed any secrets close to his heart. In some respects, however, he was categorically negative; he granted no merit to any younger writers. He acknowledged only the dead, and those few like T. S. Eliot who, though alive, were universally acknowledged. Borges had come to Europe to receive homage, but with no curiosity, no wish to discover what was new in Europe or to speak of what was new in his New World.

Borges' foreign visits have been repeated. He spent much of 1967 in the United States, giving a course at Harvard, travelling and lecturing at other places. In 1968 he visited Chile, Europe again, and Israel, where he lectured at the University of Jerusalem. The next year he was again in America, giving a course on his work at the University of Oklahoma. In 1970 he was in Brazil, the United States, France and England, and in 1971 he returned to England, where he received an honorary doctorate from Oxford University. Then, no sooner was he back in Buenos Aires than he set out again to fulfil a long held dream, and visited Iceland. He had married in 1967, but three years later he separated from his wife and returned to his mother's house. The decade was full of visits and prizes, lectures and honours. But what has been the fate of the private dreamer of the *Ficciones*, the poet who found his partial vision of God at the painted street corner in a deserted suburb of Buenos Aires?

At the beginning of the Sixties it appeared that his writing, except for an occasional short poem that he could carry in his head, had ceased. A few poems were added to the poetry volume in the collected works and in one of them he gives us a self-portrait of the private Borges, disguised under the name of Emanuel Swedenborg:

> Taller than the others, this man
> Walked among them, at a distance,
> Now and then calling the angels
> By their secret names. He would see
> That which earthly eyes do not see:
> The fierce geometry, the crystal
> Labyrinth of God . . .

> *translation by* Richard Howard and César Rennert

The Swedish engineer who had talked with angels and devils in the streets of London, finding the English uncommunicative, as Borges wryly commented, first appears in his work in a small anthology appended to the *Historia universal de la infamia*, and included in the collected works in 1954. He appears again in an anthology published by Borges and Bioy Casares in 1960. Indeed, he may be said to have given the book its name: *Libro del cielo y del infierno (Book of Heaven and Hell)*. The importance of Swedenborg for the Argentinian poet lay not only in the parallel of the tall man—Borges thinks of himself as tall—who wanders the streets of a foreign city talking with angels and devils. It lies also in the nature of these supernatural beings themselves, in the fact that in Swedenborg's eyes they are not super-natural, that they are merely men and women who have died and have chosen these shapes to fulfil their own *karma*—a term recognised by Borges but unknown to Swedenborg. The outward appearance of these beings expresses their inward state. Indeed Swedenborg's vision of a devil as a faceless man is one easily recognisable to spectators of twentieth-century politics. Borges the spectator travelled through the New World and the Old, delivering lectures, receiving prizes and honours, but all the while

> In dry Latin he went on listing
> The unconditional Last Things

> *translators* as above

The *Book of Heaven and Hell* is a treasure house of rare reading. Whereas Borges had anthologised in the past for the embellishment of his stories, he now gives his finds direct to the reader, and if several pieces in this book appear as if written by Borges, one can excuse this by saying that he has always had a rare nose for Borgesian passages in past writers.

The *Manual de zoología fantástica* (*Book of Imaginary Beings*), first published in Mexico in 1957 and ceaselessly added to until 1970, is an anthology of another kind. A work of collaboration, this time with Margarita Guerrero, it assembles imaginary creatures from the whole of past literature. But though there are some direct quotations, most of the material is recast, after the manner of the *Universal History of Infamy*. Moreover, the book is no mere ancient bestiary since it draws on writers as diverse as Sweden-borg, Kafka and C. S. Lewis. One cannot be certain that it does not contain also, under false attributions, inventions of another modern writer, Jorge Luis Borges himself. In 'Thermal Beings', a piece which appears in the complete edition, published in English as the *Book of Imaginary Beings*, we find some truly Borgesian imaginings based on a passage in the works of the German anthroposophist Rudolf Steiner.

> Mankind during the Saturnian period was a blind, deaf and insensitive multitude of articulated states of heat and cold. 'To the investigator, heat is but a substance still subtler than a gas,' we read in one page of Steiner's *Outline of Occult Science* [Borges quotes the title in German]. Before the solar stage, fire-spirits or archangels animated the bodies of those men who began to glow and shine.

The hand may sign this passage 'Rudolf Steiner', but the voice is the voice of Borges, author of 'The Circular Ruins'. Another piece, 'The Eater of the Dead', speculates on the after-life and the Judgement, citing the Egyptian and Tibetan *Books of the Dead*, and ending with a comic Egyptian passage concerning a creature that eats the souls of the unjust. Borges' bestiary is for ever encroaching on metaphysics.

Another work of collaboration, again with Bioy Casares, is *Crónicas de Bustos Domecq* (*Chronicles of Bustos Domecq*, 1967) in which this fictitious amalgam of the two lifelong friends sets up as an eater not only of the dead but of the living. The *Chronicles* reverts to an old practice of Borges, the fictitious book review. It is intended as a *sottiserie* of modern trends, but is not at its best when it takes off Robbe-Grillet's preoccupation with the objects in a room, in Bustos Domecq's case on the imaginary writer's desk. Here the parody is crude, the mockery insensitive. The best pieces are parodies of Borges' own favourite themes: the poet who reduces the whole of his experience to a single poem of a single line, and finally founds a local reputation by circulating smutty jokes; the writer who emulates Pierre Mesnard and recomposes many great works of the past, leaving an unfinished Gospel according to Saint Luke at his death. In the nicest of these self-parodies, the public, Borges' 'I' would seem to be getting the better of the secret 'I', were it not that the secret 'I' has undoubtedly taken a share in the fun. The triviality of the sillier pieces in the *Chronicles* appears to complete the separation between the public Borges and the poet, who seems to have gone into hibernation. Once a mirror for Borges held horrifying reflections, but now all mirrors seem to be shrouded and the poet to be content with the most trivial of inspiration.

9   Survival of a Poet

It is reasonable to dismiss many of the later poems of *El otro, el mismo* (*The Self and the Other*, 1969) and its two slight successors *Elogio de la sombra* (*In Praise of Darkness*, 1969) and *El oro de los tigres* (*Tigers' Gold* 1972) as occasional poems, generally well made but increasingly thin. But in each of these books there are poems of true quality on personal themes. The first of the three contains all Borges' poetry from 1930 to 1967. It therefore includes the last pieces in free verse and the poems from *El hacedor*. Such sonnets as 'Enigmas', 'A quien está leyéndome ('To my reader') and 'Everness'—a curious English title—dwell on death and survival, memory and oblivion. They free themselves from Quevedo's model and succeed in enclosing a tight metaphysical speculation in the narrow cell of fourteen lines. But the outstanding Borges' poem of the late sixties is his 'Otro poema de los dones' ('Another poem of gifts'), a piece as affirmative as his first 'Poem of gifts' was resigned. Moreover, this second poem returns to a Whitmanesque free verse, and covers more than two pages. Here it would seem that Borges varied his cerebral method of composition by working with an amanuensis or a tape-recorder. The second 'Poem of gifts' celebrates all that has given the poet joy in his life. For all these he gives thanks 'to the divine':

> For the sword and harp of the Saxons,
> For the sea, which is a shining desert
> And a secret code for things we do not know
> And an epitaph for the Norsemen,
> For the word music of England,
> For the word music of Germany,
> For gold that shines in verses,
> For epic winter . . .

translation by Alan Dugan

Before this he had enumerated many things and persons, including the now inevitable Swedenborg. The Vikings and Saxons, the gauchos and their enemies, Whitman and Francis of Assisi—all figure in Borges' list of gifts received, the last of which is 'that mysterious form of time, music.'

Borges increasingly uses free verse in *Elogio de la sombra*, the outstanding poem of which is the title piece, in which he once more considers old age and death as in the first 'Poem of gifts' he considered his blindness:

> This shadow is slow and does not hurt;
> it flows down a uniform slope
> and is like eternity.
> My friends are faceless,
> the women are what they were so many years ago . . .

Borges is striving to echo that stoic 'Epístola moral' of the seventeenth century for which he rendered thanks in 'Another poem of gifts', especially praising the poet for his anonymity, which is what he himself desired. In this poem Borges himself seems to be moving towards anonymity, confining himself to his beloved *topoi* and striking no metaphors of his own. Another piece in this book, also one of the best, treats of death in a more personal way. It is a prose poem with an English title that recalls Eliot, 'His end and his beginning'; and in it, once more as in the stories of his early years, transcendence is associated with pain and fear. He dreams that he is dead, and that the things he is aware of are only echoes and shadows, which he knows he must abandon. He has earned grace and ever since his death has been in heaven. But to accustom himself to this new and alien world is horrible. In another prose poem 'La oración' ('Prayer') Borges justifies petitionary prayer by a twisted Borgesian argument. These pieces fall outside the bounds of poetry; they mark the attempts of an aging man to find an acceptable metaphysic for which he can exchange his old heretical scepticism.

El oro de los tigres shows a falling off in the poet, and an increasing tendency to let the verses carry the poem. Yet here, too, there are occasional memories, as in 'El Centinela' ('The Sentinel'), of the old divided poet who wakes at morning to assume the human condition and take on the burdens of that other Borges who

> . . . lies in wait for me in mirrors, in (shining)
>   mahogany, in shop windows' glass.
> Some woman or another has repulsed him and I must
>   share his grief.
> Now he is dictating this poem to me, which does not
>   please me.
> He compels me to my nebulous apprenticeship to
>   Anglo-Saxon, a tough language.
> He has converted me to an idolatrous worship of dead
>   soldiers with whom I could probably not exchange
>   a single word.

Finally he turns on the other who 'drinks the water from his cup and devours his bread.' The end is despairing:

> The door of suicide is open, but the theologians affirm
>   that in the further shadow of the other kindom I
>   shall be waiting for me.

It is an old man's poetry, written not with the rare old man's passion that inspired Yeats, but with a muted fear and horror, and with regret, as in the title poem, for the gold of a woman's hair that his hands once longed for.

If the last two volumes of poetry represent a decline in Borges' inspiration, this is counteracted by a new collection of stories which appeared in 1971, *El informe de Brodie* (*Doctor Brodie's Report*). He himself describes it as 'a set of modest experiments in straightforward story-telling', and has explained in interviews that he no longer cares to write metaphysical tales since his younger imitators have taken this task from him and he prefers to attempt something new. This book was probably completed by the middle Sixties. But he talks of still more work in production including a long story called 'The Congress' that suggests Kafka, but which he hopes will turn out more in the line of Chesterton.

The best of the dozen stories in *Doctor Brodie's Report* are in fact the least straightforward and the most closely related to his old vein. The story 'Guayaquil' describes a contest between two professors as to which is to undertake a sponsored journey to transcribe certain newly discovered documents. Borges compares it with a magical contest between two sorcerers which he quotes from the *Mabinogion*. Here we have the academic contest, and the magical one. But between them is sandwiched another: the letters that occasion the first were exchanged by the two rival 'liberators' of Spanish America, Bolivar and San Martín. The story is told by the defeated professor, who is uncomfortably conscious of the survival of magic in the modern world. For he feels that he has been forced to resign the coveted journey to Sulaco, Joseph Conrad's city in *Nostromo*, by no 'natural' means. Another story of rivalry, 'El duelo' (The Duel') attempts a theme more suitable to Henry James than to Borges. His suggestion that the true battle was not that between the two lady painters, but between one of them and another lady who remains in the background, fails because he misses dramatic possibilities that James would have seized on. The third lady remains shadowy throughout, and the plot is consequently a skeleton only partially clothed in flesh.

'Literature is nothing but a directed dream,' wrote Borges in the introduction to this book, which contains several perhaps only partially directed nightmares. Two gaucho brothers kill the girl with whom they are both in love because their obsession with her has come between them. Two men, gauchos also, so loathe one another that they are in conflict even in the competitive courage with which they face execution. A hideous suggestion of the violence in seemingly innocent men is contained in the story of some up country farmers who, hearing for the first time an account of the crucifixion from a travelling student, re-enact it, compelling him to take the part of Christ. Impersonal violence is the theme of another story in which two daggers in a showcase, once the property of famous gauchos, force two young middle-class men to wield them in a fight to the death that neither of them desires. But the boy narrator of the incident follows the duel with excited admiration. Courage also dazzles the Jewish boy of another tale, who worships a local thief for his vaunted courage, and when he finds that the man is no hero, callously betrays him to the police. Only one story in the book points the opposite moral. The man who mysteriously refused to kill in Borges' first story 'The Man at the Pink Corner' returns to explain his reasons for refusing the fight. He saw in his opponent, he explains, a mirror portrait of himself, a violent bully, and was ashamed. Therefore he walked away, to live the rest of his life as an obscure nobody.

The subtle violence of personal rivalry and the overt violence of primitive men are the subjects of most of the stories in this book. The title piece, 'Doctor Brodie's Report', carries the theme to its culmination. The Scottish doctor reports on a primitive tribe newly discovered by him, which reveres poets. 'He is not a man but a son of god', they cry, 'and anyone may kill him.' One may read this as a protest by the 'other', public Borges, lionised on American campuses, and in danger of being torn apart by enthusiastic ladies' clubs. Worship of poets is more pleasant to the outward personage than to the creator within.

Doctor Brodie's Report, then, is a book of not so straightforward tales told with some of the involutions of *Ficciones*. The language is plainer, the allusions fewer, and once more, in the introduction, Borges renounces his long-discarded cult of *lunfardo*, the thieves' slang of Buenos Aires. The most suitable words are for him now the most current throughout the Spanish-speaking world. Yet these stories, like his earlier ones, remain absolutely of the New World. They could not be mistaken, either in theme, language or viewpoint, for anything written in Spain. Had they appeared first in English, however, but for their lack of sexuality they might have been taken for the work of an unknown American writer, a disciple of the early William Faulkner who had read the *Ficciones* of the Argentinian Jorge Luis Borges.

10 Borges in his World

Borges' position in the world of letters is much and bitterly dis-
puted. On the one hand, he appears to be an original writer in
the tradition of the European decadence, whose private imaginings embody a true freedom: the ranging freedom of intellectual
speculation. This is the face that he turns to Europe. This is the
Borges who is fêted on the American campuses, and who is the
subject of innumerable doctoral theses. As such, he will possibly
be awarded the Nobel prize this year or next.

Yet in Europe and America his chief readers are among the
young, for whom he expresses an existential anxiety, a questioning
of the values and reality of life itself. It is the young, not the conservative old, who buy him in paperback, who quote him and see
in his nightmares a recognisable counterpart to their own.
Borges, the Argentinian oligarch, who has lately dedicated his
Whitman translation to President Nixon, is put beside Tolkien
and the writers of science fiction as a master of the 'directed
dream'. For these young readers, he is an a-political figure, a pure
creator. His scholarly references, genuine or invented, are seen as
pure fantasy; his tricks with time and eternity convey the true
thrill to readers who, like Borges, are no longer convinced by plain
clock time and naturalistic explanations. Borges readmits magic
at an intellectual level. Perhaps the rival Presidents of the super-
powers, red and star-spangled, are indeed the sorcerers of the
Mabinogion, revived to fight out their old duel in new clothes and
with weapons only to be controlled by the hideousness of their
own fears.

On the other hand, in the Spanish New World to which he
essentially belongs Borges is a controversial figure, as much disliked—though he is seldom denigrated—by younger writers as he
is admired by the young in Europe and America. In their eyes, he

is the great ancestor who has betrayed his people, the father who denies his sons.

'His dazzling prose,' writes the Mexican novelist Carlos Fuentes in a small book on the new novèl in Spanish America, 'so cold that it burns the lips, is the first to put us in connection, to draw us from our hovels and throw us out into the world, to which it relates us without diminishing us. It gives us reality. For the final meaning of Borges' prose—without which there would simply be no modern Spanish-American novel—is that it bears witness that Latin America has no language and must create one.'

Fuentes' accent on linguistics, on the need for new language, is exaggerated. Borges writes a clear Spanish that has undergone the discipline of much English reading. But Borges has given a much more important incentive to the birth of the new novel: he has readmitted all the resources of myth. Before Borges, the Latin American novel was preoccupied with social questions; it was political, naturalistic and extremely dull. The Spanish American novelist either attempted European themes, transplanting Gide, Joyce or Virginia Woolf to their New World, or meticulously documented that new world, its rubber forests, its fisheries, the rivalries of its landowners, the oppression of its peasants. But the young men who learned from Borges returned to myth, the quality that united them with the Indians and consequently with a land that was still steeped in myth, that was only marginally European-ised. Fuentes himself, in his first book of stories, *Los días enmascarados* (*Masked days*), tells a Borges-like story of the god who invented rain and took refuge in the cellar of a house, where he was discovered by the narrator; and indeed his finest novel, *La muerte de Artemio Cruz* (*The Death of Artemio Cruz*) turns time upside down in a Borgesian manner. Fuentes, however, was an early disciple who came to value Borges principally for his language; he has latterly become a disciple of the American novelists and of D. H. Lawrence, preferring far ranging sexual and pseudo-mystical description to the small-scale annotations with which he began.

Julio Cortázar, a fellow Argentinian, has throughout his career admired Borges, whose influence remains present in his very different work. He is said to keep Borges' photograph on the walls of his study, though the master has long ago renounced the pupil, if he ever acknowledged him. Certainly Cortázar's first published story appeared in a short-lived periodical edited by Borges, and the signature of the master is noticeable not only in Cortázar's early stories, but in whole passages of his most important work, the novel *Rayuela* (*Hopscotch*). Early stories by Cortázar that were inspired by Borges tell of a tiger that roamed a patrician house in Argentina, of a man who by dint of gazing at an axolotl in an aquarium tank became an axolotl; reality is for ever shading off into mystery, the present and the past have their secret correspondences. *Hopscotch* is a novel of far broader conception that Borges could ever have devised. Yet in it, particularly in those parts that bring the protagonists (or their doubles) back from Paris to Buenos Aires, there are repeated reminiscences of the master. Borges is specially present in that scene in which the characters play their mysterious game of hopscotch in the courtyard of a madhouse, a scene in which each move from darkness into light and back again suggests a mysterious Borgesian dance oɪ cross significances. And even later, in his wry sketches of mythical beasts, *Historias de cronopios y famas*, Cortázar is developing in a quite individual way the theme of imaginary beings adumbrated by Borges in his zoological fantasies. It is true that Cortázar has drawn on surrealism, a contemporary heresy to which Borges has never subscribed. He acknowledges his debt to the master. But the master responds only with a snide sneer at the 'disciples' who now write his stories for him, compelling him to change his subjects and treatments.

Not only Cortázar but Gabriel García Márquez, the Colombian novelist of *Cien años de soledad* (*A Hundred Years of Solitude*), owes a debt to Borges. Indeed, in Borges' sense, *Cien años* may be described as an allegory, and would therefore be exempted from his general condemnation of the naturalistic novel, which attempts to explain effects by causes. García Márquez, moreover, has an epic sweep that can be seen as a vast magnification of those concentrated passages, in stories such as 'The Theologians' or 'The Lottery in Babylon', in which Borges sketches a whole historical development by the cunning assemblage of a few symbolic details. In a recent interview (*The Observer* colour supplement, 10 December 1972) García Márquez stated that fourteen volumes of Borges' works were among the few books that he kept permanently with him in his various changes of domicile.

But if Borges is the father of this generation which began to write in the Fifties and which has made the Spanish–American novel one of the most interesting developments in modern literature, he shows no awareness of the fact. When asked for the names of modern younger writers, he answers that there are none. His attitude towards the next generation, like that of the whole *Sur* group, is that of Ibsen's *Master Builder*. They may knock at the door, but in vain; the covers of *Sur* are closed against them. For Victoria Ocampo and her group the 'revolution of 1955' is the last event in history. It put the oligarchs back into power, making the world safe for their conservative culture. For them Perón was a reincarnation of the 'tyrant' Rosas, and any progressive movement in Spanish America threatens a fresh tyranny.

But after the revolution of 1955 came the Cuban revolution of 1959, a new Peronism in their world, of which Batista's Havana had been a cultural pearl. They publicly proclaimed their opposition to Fidel Castro as they had to their own 'tyrant' and sent messages of support to the Cuban exiles who landed at Playa Girón to 'liberate' their 'oppressed' country. Victoria Ocampo indeed dismissed José Bianco, for long the responsible editor of *Sur*, for voicing, with many other Argentinian intellectuals, his support for Fidel Castro and for visiting Cuba.

Why, one may ask, did Borges publicly identify himself with a political issue that did not concern his country? He is said to have attempted an intercession for Bianco. But to no purpose: he had committed himself to the party of the embattled mandarins and antagonised the majority of the best writers in Spanish America, who were guardedly or wholeheartedly in favour of Fidel Castro's revolution and of Cuba's declaration of independence from the Americans.

A leading Marxist critic, the Cuban poet Roberto Fernández Retamar, has attempted to put the Borges 'scandal'—as he calls it—in a wider context. In the nineteenth century, the intellectuals of the semi-colonial countries of America saw themselves in terms of a social triangle suggested to them by Shakespeare's *Tempest*. They were Ariel and would break the spell of Prospero, the exploiting powers, to free Caliban, the vast native population.

Their weapon could be education, the panacea advocated by the Argentinian Sarmiento, whom Borges greatly admires. What part the United States would play was in the nineteenth century undecided. The Cuban poet José Martí saw the Americans as the principal oppressors; others expected American help in combating the British and French Prospero.

The young Borges had been an anti-imperialist. Retamar quotes from an essay of his written in 1926.

> 'I want to speak to the creoles, to the men who feel that they live in this country, not to those who believe that the sun and the moon are in Europe. This is a land of born exiles, of people nostalgic for the far away, and foreign. They are the true *gringos*, whether their blood is autochthonous or not, and to them my pen does not speak.'

The voice is authentic Borges, even to a couple of Argentinianisms which are not in the dictionary. It was at this time that he spoke of the 'barbarous' northern neighbour. Against this Retamar quotes a statement of Borges in 1955: 'I believe that Europe is our tradition.' This, in Retamar's view, is a betrayal, a deliberate change of idea induced by the flattery of honours and recognition. And Retamar continues his attack on the treacherous Ariels by accusing Cortázar, Fuentes and others of the next generation for not supporting the Cuban revolution uncritically.

Such an attack might seem to demand no refutation, were it not that its few literary—as distinct from political—statements contain a kernel of truth. It would be unjust to attribute Borges' *volte-face* between 1926 and 1955 to social pressures or temptations. 'Borges,' Retamar says grudgingly, 'writes a Spanish that it is difficult to read without admiration. He is no madman, but on the contrary extremely lucid. He exemplifies Martí's conception of the intelligence, which is one part of a man and not the best.' In another part of his essay, Retamar stresses the narrowness of Borges' interests—in dreams, mirrors, labyrinths, violence and learning—which are the hallmarks of his Europeanised decadence.

Retamar is not alone in attacking the narrowness of Borges'

interests, and the angry conservatism of his judgements. It is a weakness that nowhere in the stories do we find any concern with character, any reflections on love, indeed any women considered as such and not as the object of a vain yearning masculine senti-ment, nor any children. His intellectualism repels the very intellectual Retamar. An equally destructive attack on Borges and his 'transcendental game' is made by the Argentinian critic Blas Matamoro who, with the backing of a friendly psycho-analyst, lays the unhappy writer on the professional couch. The symbolism of the stories is made to reveal a classical Oedipus complex. Borges desired his mother, fostered a secret and guilty hatred for his father. Labyrinths are interpreted as womb sym-bols, and the dagger as an angry phallus. At his most exaggera-tive, Sr. Matamoro sees the chess game at the opening of 'The Secret Miracle' as a phallic battle between the Borges, father and son, who play sixteen-a-side. Both the writing and the political attitudes of the poet are explained as symptoms of his psychologi-cal peculiarities, and he is condemned with a degree of venom quite foreign to the deliberate neutrality of Freud himself.

A better, because more temperate, case against Borges is made by the Mexican critic Jaime García Terrés, who has no political prejudice against him: 'My general complaint is that in Borges I find the perfected perversity of an inhibited mind, turned in on itself, a sort of self-sufficient vacuum.' This was written in 1955, under the impact of the *Ficciones*. 'The creative adventure,' he goes on, 'does not go beyond the inventive process, and furnishes nothing but further arid mechanisms. His characters have neither soul nor body. They are merely names set in relation to other names.'

Without excusing Borges' narrow and often ill-natured con-servatism or the intellectual coldness of his narratives, even of his poems, it is possible to make a case for his enduring achievement which will bypass the often valid strictures of the Marxists, of the progressive writers like Fuentes, and of less committed judges like García Terrés.

In the first place, Borges stands, as Fuentes and many others have affirmed, as the father, the 'great Inca', of the modern Spanish American novel. Confronting the problem of language, peninsular or Argentinian, traditional or colloquial, he has achieved an idiom that even his bitterest detractors admire: an idiom deeply influenced by the English authors he loves and rigorous after the fashion of Latin in its grammatical clarity. All the critics I have cited in this chapter present problems of translation; they use abstract nouns of imprecise meaning, and make statements that wander round the point. By contrast, any sentence by Borges is crystalline; its only fault is that sometimes it expresses too much in too little space.

But in a poet and storyteller, linguistic mastery is not enough. It is true that the characters in his stories have 'neither soul nor body' that they are no more than chessmen on a metaphysical board. They are his pawns in a game he is playing without human opponent. He makes all the moves. The two parties may be labelled gaucho and soldier, police and robber, the 'Company' and the individual, the Minotaur and his slayer, the spy and the professor. Always one will stand for death, the other for a possible life, one for dream and the other for a dubious reality. And always the manipulator of the pieces will favour the side of death and dream, while comforting the losers with the hope that perhaps somewhere, on the farther side of death or waking, there may be for them the chance of ultimate victory. Retamar reproaches Borges for thus being on the side of death or, in his terms, of reaction.

It is certainly true that Borges ignores the burning social issues of his times, and almost mechanically rejects anything that belongs to the world of the last fifty years. Even on the metaphysical side, he avoids issues. He thinks no problem to its conclusion, always stepping back to shelter behind a dry irony. He is the supreme example of the escapist, who fails to make good his escape. His dryness conveys a total rejection of all positive values, but therein lies his strength. For total rejection of both God and man is terrible.

A reader who accepts the possibility of transcendence expressed by all religions may pity Borges for his constant rejection of the many shreds of evidence to the existence which he testifies in his stories and poems. But this is no more valid a criticism than that of the Marxists. One cannot reproach him for refusing his many 'intimations of immortality', or for his retreat into labyrinthine intellectualism. The value of the stories lies in their highly original 'mechanisms'—to borrow García Terrés' phrase—and in their accurate portrayal of a human situation that is common—though in lesser concentration than we find in Borges—throughout the Western world. Borges embodies the would-be believer who cannot trust his nascent belief, the Pascalian waverer who cannot make the leap into faith. The essence of his irony is its self-protective intention, and its failure really to protect. For Borges continues to walk the streets of his city talking, like Swedenborg, with angels, but assuring them and us that they are the fictions of the other Borges, which fail to convince the public Borges of their authenticity. All his life Borges has wished to be convinced of some reality, of the reality of culture, of the reality of his city, of his country, of his ancestral line. In saying that 'Europe is our tradition' he has betrayed no political faith, but he has betrayed himself: his own quest for authentiticy, which cannot find its grail in Europe or on an American campus.

Borges is an essentially American figure. All the great writers of America, Spanish or English by language, have been in quest of their tradition. Some, like Henry James, Melville, Hawthorne, Ezra Pound, Eliot have attached themselves to Europe, constantly invoking an English or multilingual culture to which they wished to belong. Native born European writers have been less self-conscious about their heritage and ancestry.

Of Spanish American writers, most before Borges have loosely attached themselves to the French tradition. Until at least the Twenties Paris was the cultural capital of Spanish America. Borges preferred London. But the next generation look rather to the older writers of America, to the novelists of the U.S.A., to one or two great poets writing in Spanish, the chief among them being César Vallejo, Vicente Huidobro and Pablo Neruda—and to Jorge Luis Borges, admired and maligned, a consummate master of his own restricted territory and on that account a writer only a little less than great.

Bibliography

1   Translations

Labyrinths London (Penguin Books) 1970; (New Directions Publishing Corporation) 1962, 1964. A good introductory anthology.

A Personal Anthology London (Jonathan Cape) 1968; (Picador) 1972. Borges' own selection.

Ficciones New York (Grove Press); London (Weidenfeld and Nicolson) (Calder Books) 1962. Translation of Spanish collection of that name.

The Aleph London (Jonathan Cape) 1971. Another anthology with notes and a brief autobiography by Borges written in English. This selection is complementary to *Labyrinths*, and does not correspond to the Spanish book of the same name.

Selected Poems 1923–1967 London (Allen Lane, The Penguin Press) 1972. Bilingual selection with notes.

The Book of Imaginary Beings London (Jonathan Cape) 1970. The most complete version of this miscellany of imaginary creatures.

Dreamtigers Austin, U.S.A. (University of Texas Press) 1964, New York (Dutton) 1970. A translation of the Spanish volume *El Hacedor*.

Other Inquisitions Austin, U.S.A. (University of Texas Press) New York (Simon and Schuster) 1965. Translation of essays, *Otras Inquisicones*

The Spanish Language in South America—a Literary Problem and (in Spanish), *El Gaucho Martín Fierro*. (The Hispanic Council 1964). Two lectures given in England.

Extraordinary Tales, written in collaboration with Bioy Casares, London (Souvenir Press) 1973.

A Universal History of Infamy New York (Dutton) 1972; London (Allen Lane, The Penguin Press) 1973.

2   Spanish editions of works by Borges at present obtainable

(a) *Poetry.*

Fervor de Buenos Aires Buenos Aires (Imprenata Serantes) 1923.
Luna de Enfrente (with *Cuaderno San Martín*) Buenos Aires (Proa) 1925 and 1929.
El Otro, El Mismo, 1969; *Elogio de la Sombra,* 1969; *El Oro de Los Tigres,* Buenos Aires (uniform edition, all Emecé) 1972.
Poemas Escogidos Barcelona (Ocnos) 1972. A satisfactory selection.

(b) *Stories.*

Ficciones Buenos Aires (*Sur*) 1945; (Emecé) 1956.
El Aleph Buenos Aires (Volumes of the *Obras completas,* Emecé) 1957; Madrid (Alianza).
El Informe de Brodie Buenos Aires (*Obras completas,* Emecé); Barcelona (Plaza y Jamés) 1971.
Historia Universal de la Infamia Barcelona (*Obras Completas,* Emecé) 1954; Barcelona (Alianza and Plaza y Jamés) 1971.

(c) *Essays and Miscellaneous prose.*

Evaristo Carriego Buenos Aires (Geizer) 1930; Buenos Aires (Emecé) 1955.
Historia de la Eternidad Madrid (Alianza) 1971.
Discusión Buenos Aires (*Obras completas,* Emecé) 1957.
Otras Inquisiciones Buenos Aires (*Obras completas,* Emecé) 1960.
El Hacedor A miscellany. Buenos Aires, (*Obras completas,* Emecé) 1960.
Leopoldo Lugones, segunda edicion Buenos Aires (Troquel) 1955; Buenos Aires (Pleamar) 1965.

(d) *Anthologies.*

Nueva Antologia Personal, Buenos Aires (Emecé). Borges own selection.

(e) *Books written in collaboration with Adolfo Bioy Casares.*

Seis Problemas Para Don Isidro Parodi by Bustos Domecq. Buenos Aires (*Sur*) 1942.

Cuentes brevis y extraordinarios, Buenos Aires (Rueda) 1967.

Crónicas de Bustos Domecq Buenos Aires (Losada) 1967.

Libro del Cielo y del Infierno Buenos Aires (*Sur*) 1960; Barcelona (Libros de Bolsillo, Edhasa) 1971.

3 Critical Works on aspects of Borges' work

Guillermo Sucre: *Borges El Poeta* Venezuela (Monte Avila Editores, Caracas) 1968. Excellent criticism.

Néstor Ibarra: *Borges et Borges* Paris (L'Herme) 1969. Gossipy, personal and occasionally illuminating.

César Fernández Moreno: *Esquema de Borges* Buenos Aires (Perrot) 1957. Useful for the early years.

Saul Yurkievich; *Fundadores de la Nueva Poesia Latino américana* Barcelona (Barrel Editores) 1971. Perceptive essay on Borges as 'poeta circular'.

Marcos Ricardo Baratán: *Jorge Luis Borges* Madrid (Ediciones Jucar) 1972. An anthology of poems with critical introduction.

Ronald J. Christ: *The Narrow Act, Borges' Art of Allusion.* (University of London Press, and New York University Press) 1969. An academic study of restricted scope.

Carter Wheelock: *The Mythmaker* Austin, U.S.A. (University of Texas Press)1969. Extracts astonishing symbolisms from Borges' stories. Borges himself wrote the most elegant letter of thanks for 'this beautiful book . . . in which you have penetrated so intimately into my mind'.

Jaime Alazraki: *Jorge Luis Borges* New York, (Columbia University Press) 1971. A simple introductory essay.

Blas Matamoro: *Jorge Luis Borges, El Juego Transcendente* Buenos Aires (Pena Lino) 1971. See chapter 10 of this book.

These are but a few of the studies of Borges, academic and otherwise, that have appeared in the English and Spanish speaking countries in recent years.